**Also by Mary D. Esselman and
Elizabeth Ash Vélez**

*Hell with Love: Poems to Mend a Broken Heart*

*Kiss Off: Poems to Set You Free*

*You Drive Me Crazy: Love Poems for Real Life*

# HOW DI

# THIS HAPP

# HOW DID THIS HAPPEN?

POEMS FOR THE NOT SO YOUNG ANYMORE

MARY D. ESSELMAN AND
ELIZABETH ASH VÉLEZ

**GRAND CENTRAL**
PUBLISHING

NEW YORK   BOSTON   NASHVILLE

Grand Central Publishing
Hachette Book Group
1290 Avenue of the Americas
New York, NY 10104

www.GrandCentralPublishing.com

First Edition: April 2017

Grand Central Publishing is a division of Hachette Book Group, Inc.
The Grand Central Publishing name and logo is a trademark of Hachette Book
Group, Inc.

The Hachette Speakers Bureau provides a wide range of authors for speak-
ing events. To find out more, go to www.HachetteSpeakersBureau.com or call
(866) 376-6591.

The publisher is not responsible for websites (or their content) that are not owned
by the publisher.

Library of Congress Cataloging-in-Publication Data is available upon request.

ISBN 978-1-4555-6700-3 (hardcover edition)
ISBN 978-1-4555-6699-0 (ebook edition)

Printed in the United States of America

LSC-C

10 9 8 7 6 5 4 3 2 1

# Contents

Introduction                                                    *xiii*

## Insult
### (WHEN YOU DON'T RECOGNIZE YOURSELF IN THE MIRROR)

A FOUND POEM
DISCOVERED IN A SARAH
SILVERMAN TWEET             42 AND Female                    15

ARIWARA NO NARIHIRA        That It Is a Road                16

DEBORAH LANDAU             Solitaire                        17

FAITH SHEARIN              Being Called Ma'am               20

CHANA BLOCH                Tired Sex                        22

JENNIFER TONGE             Self-Portrait at 38              23

SYLVIA PLATH               Mirror                           25

NATALIE WISE               Tell Us a Story, Grandma         27

_v_

# CONTENTS

| RODDY LUMSDEN | The Young | 28 |
| EURIPIDES | From *Herakles* | 30 |
| SHARON OLDS | 35/10 | 31 |
| A.E. HOUSMAN | Into my heart an air that kills | 32 |
| EMILY DICKINSON | The difference between Despair | 33 |

# Injury
## (WHEN YOU REALIZE AGING IS A THING)

| ADELAIDE CRAPSEY | November Night | 51 |
| MOIRA EGAN | What the Flesh Is Heir To | 52 |
| WILLIAM BUTLER YEATS | The Balloon of the Mind | 53 |
| GERARD MANLEY HOPKINS | I wake and feel the fell of dark, not day | 54 |
| MOIRA EGAN | Not Flashing but Waving | 56 |
| JO MCDOUGALL | Mammogram | 57 |

| | | |
|---|---|---|
| LINDA PASTAN | At the Gynecologist's | *58* |
| ERIC RAWSON | At Fifty | *59* |
| DEBORAH LANDAU | Minutes, Years | *61* |
| DEBORAH GARRISON | A Human Calculation | *63* |
| DEVIN JOHNSTON | Fixed Interval | *65* |
| GAIL MAZUR | Why You Travel | *66* |
| HORACE | From *Epodes* | *68* |
| FRANÇOIS VILLON | From *The Testament* | *70* |
| GERARD MANLEY HOPKINS | Pied Beauty | *71* |
| WARSAN SHIRE | what they did yesterday afternoon | *72* |
| EMILY DICKINSON | Down Time's quaint stream | *74* |

# Defiance
### (WHEN YOU THINK YOU CAN MAKE IT ALL GO AWAY)

| | | |
|---|---|---|
| DOROTHY PARKER | Indian Summer | *92* |
| RAINER MARIA RILKE | You see, I want a lot | *93* |

# CONTENTS

MELISSA BRODER — Gold Lipstick and the End of Summer — 94

JANE HIRSHFIELD — The Bearded Woman — 95

LUCILLE CLIFTON — there is a girl inside — 96

GAIUS LUCILIUS — Wig, rouge, honey — 98

AMY POEHLER — Selected "Plastic Surgery Haiku" — 99

EMILY DICKINSON — Much Madness is divinest Sense — 101

A FOUND POEM DISCOVERED IN AN INTERVIEW WITH FRANCES MCDORMAND — Laugh Lines — 102

ANNE SHELDON — Snow White Turns 39 — 104

MARGE PIERCY — To be of use — 105

CLAUDIA EMERSON — Lifeguard — 107

ANNE BOYER — what resembles the grave but isn't — 109

# Dread
## (WHEN YOU REALIZE YOU CAN'T EVEN)

DEBORAH LANDAU — I Don't Have a Pill for That — 125

| JANE HIRSHFIELD | Bruises | 127 |
| LOUISE GLÜCK | Matins | 128 |
| MEGHAN O'ROURKE | Ever | 129 |
| KELLY CHERRY | Lines Written on the Eve of a Birthday | 131 |
| MARGARET ATWOOD | Porcupine Meditation | 132 |
| ZHU SHUZHEN | Waking Up | 134 |
| DOROTHY PARKER | Coda | 135 |
| LUCILLE CLIFTON | it was a dream | 136 |
| THEODORE ROETHKE | "Long Live the Weeds" | 137 |

# Grit

### (WHEN YOU FIND A WAY TO LIVE WITH YOURSELF)

| | From the *Sutta Nipata* | 152 |
| RITA DOVE | Dawn Revisited | 153 |
| DEREK WALCOTT | Love After Love | 154 |
| EDWARD FIELD | People Who Eat in Coffee Shops | 155 |

CONTENTS

| | | |
|---|---|---|
| JASON SCHNEIDERMAN | sugar is smoking | *156* |
| ELIZABETH ASH VÉLEZ | Caroline County | *157* |
| JANE HIRSHFIELD | Mele in Gabbia | *158* |
| CAROLYN CREEDON | Woman, Mined | *159* |
| BARBARA CROOKER | Strewn | *161* |
| BARBARA RAS | A Wife Explains Why She Likes Country | *163* |
| GRACE PALEY | Walking in the Woods | *165* |
| GWENDOLYN BROOKS | Old Mary | *166* |
| MARIE HOWE | What the Living Do | *167* |
| FRANK O'HARA | Today | *169* |
| EMILY DICKINSON | I dwell in Possibility | *170* |

# Grace
### (WHEN YOU FIND A WAY TO LIVE IN THE WORLD)

| | | |
|---|---|---|
| JULIE WILLIAMS | Coming Up Into the Light | *189* |
| MARIE HOWE | The Gate | *190* |
| JAMES WRIGHT | Milkweed | *192* |

| SEAMUS HEANEY | Postscript | 193 |
| ADA LIMÓN | The Conditional | 194 |
| RUTH STONE | Green Apples | 195 |
| THOMAS LUX | A Little Tooth | 196 |
| WILLIAM SHAKESPEARE | From *The Tempest* | 197 |
| WALT WHITMAN | From *Song of Myself* | 198 |
| CLIVE JAMES | Japanese Maple | 199 |
| WALLACE STEVENS | Of Mere Being | 201 |
| MARGARET ATWOOD | Solstice Poem, iv | 202 |
| GRACE PALEY | Here | 204 |

| Authors' Note and Afterword | 207 |
| Permissions | 211 |
| Citations | 223 |
| Acknowledgments | 229 |

# Introduction

*Every so often I read a book about age, and whoever's writing it says it's great to be old. It's great to be wise and sage and mellow; it's great to be at the point where you understand just what matters in life. I can't stand people who say things like this.*

—NORA EPHRON

This book is for every woman who has faced "OMG, how did this happen?" moments of aging, from ego-gutting recognitions (your mother's face stares out from your previously reliable bathroom mirror) to nerve-shredding indignities (there are few hours in life less agreeable than those dedicated to the ceremony known as a mammogram—except the ones dedicated to the colonoscopy). And worse.

This is forty and then some. This is aging: something that happens to other people, until it happens to you. That gray hair. Those apple cheeks puddling into jowls. To bother with vanity or (pretend to) ignore it? The pap smear scare. Cold sweat at the doctor's and hot flashes at night. Issues cosmetic and cosmic—but wait, how did this happen?

Five minutes ago, give or take a decade, we were thirty-somethings, flexing our way through dating and heartbreak and work drama, building careers and planning weddings, running marathons and swaddling babies—and now? You, who used to flinch at the sight of the grisly Dansko women in the Whole Foods parking lot, you, who blithely sprinted past the walking wounded on the track at the gym—here you are now, Birkenstock-shod in the supplements section, straining to read the ingredients labels, or post knee surgery in the Yoga for Healing class, hoarding blankets and vigilantly guarding your spot from pesky latecomers.

It simply cannot be. And yet somehow here we are, discovering the fight-or-flight hell that is "aging while female," a vexing side effect of what writer Olivia Laing calls the "perpetual, harrowing, nonconsensual beauty pageant of femininity." We struggle to transition from freaked-out to fabulous but find ourselves caught between revulsion and pride, fear and fortitude, the need to appear "professional" and "attractive" and the desire to resist social norms that equate "professional and attractive" with "young and hot."

Let's face it: getting from the shock (is that my face?!) to the awe (Viola Davis on the red carpet) of growing older requires emotional grace, intellectual grit, an expert dermatologist, and the company of true friends. Even then there's no guarantee you'll move from "I feel bad about my neck!" to "I'm an iconic badass!" But chances are you'll find equanimity, even joy, on your journey.

We can't provide the expert dermatologist, but we can offer a way to cultivate that grace, grit, and camaraderie, through a book that does for aging what we did for heartbreak in *The Hell with Love: Poems to Mend a Broken Heart*: guide, amuse, and comfort women who are going through a major life change—this time the natural but often deeply disruptive process of growing older. Through poetry—yes, hilarious, fierce poetry, from Gwendolyn Brooks to Amy Poehler—you'll find commiseration and inspiration to carry you through pivotal phases of aging:

Insult
(When you don't recognize yourself in the mirror)

Injury
(When you realize aging is a thing)

Defiance
(When you think you can make it all go away)

Dread
(When you realize you can't even)

Grit
(When you find a way to live with yourself)

Grace
(When you find a way to live in the world)

So many of us experience aging alone, unprepared and unwilling to face it, from that first sneak attack to many dark nights of the soul. Despite our cheerful Facebook feeds, we're confused and embarrassed, grieving what's lost, afraid of what's to come, and unsure of how to move forward. (Try to get all that across in an emoji.) We'll take you through this journey together, in company that's safe and wise, funny and supportive.

And who, you may ask, are "we," daring to accompany you through aging, mixing our words with those of poetic geniuses like Lucille Clifton, Sylvia Plath, and Ada Limón? We're Mary, fifty-four, and Elizabeth, seventy-one, longtime best friends who love literature (we're both teachers) and pop culture (both former *People* magazine reporters) and who for the past thirty years have helped each other make sense of the world, one poem or *Broad City* episode at a time.

When late motherhood and right-on-time perimenopause collided for Mary, she searched in vain for a book or website that would "get" what she was going through, something that faced aging head-on, with smarts, humor, irony, and cold, hard truth. Nothing that screamed MENOPAUSE, INFIRMITY, DEATH, but nothing delusional about the wonders of decrepitude: "Oh, the fragrant wisdom of old age, musty with self-knowledge, I inhale it with gusto!" No. All she wanted was something relatable and real, not *Ten Top Tips for Tip-Top Aging*, not *Look At My Gorgeous Over-40 Ass* books by ex-models and celebrities. Where, oh where was her *Are You There God? It's Me, Perimenopausal Margaret?*

Elizabeth weighed in: "A little wine every night, a little Celexa every morning, and Valium as needed—oh, and Toni Morrison every day." And while drug-phobic Mary rejected booze and meds, she did find solace and strength in Elizabeth's doses of pop-literary therapy, from Margaret Atwood to Samantha Bee. And so: this book was born, a poetic how-to for women growing older, rooted in the wisdom of great thinkers and writers.

We aim to weave together our cultural experience of aging with poems that can help us cope. Because what's so different, really, between Emily Dickinson's steely truth telling and Amy Schumer's brilliant feminism, or Dorothy Parker's devastating wit and Lena Dunham's unapologetic frankness? They all evince an *attitude* toward aging, a female point of view that celebrates the Grace Paley–meets–Melissa McCarthy approach: "We are here, we exist, we are beautiful and gross and human; we grow up, and we grow old, and so what?"

One reason Schumer has struck such a chord with women of all ages is that she speaks truth to the power of sexism in our culture. We can all laugh at Schumer, Tina Fey, and Patricia Arquette sending Julia Louis-Dreyfus up the river after celebrating her last "fuckable" day (in the now classic sketch) because we know it's true: after "a certain age," women become invisible in our culture—unless they avail themselves of the subterfuge that writer Jennifer Weiner lamented in a *New York Times* op-ed: "How do you preach the gospel of body positivity when you're breathless from your Spanx? How can you tell your girls that inner beauty matters when you're texting them the message from your aesthetician's chair?" As Weiner said of the pressure to age pretty, "It's sexist, and depressing, and expensive, costly in terms of both money and time."

And that's where this book comes in, a guide for when you don't have the time, money, or comedic company of Schumer's merry menoposse. A poem is free therapy you can access anytime, like a prayer or a song. The best poems, the ones that stick with you, console you when you're grieving and steel you when you're scared—they "get" you, your weirdness and fears and inside jokes, just like a best friend, and they won't walk away when you lash out or melt down. Pick up these poems when you wake, sweating, at two a.m. and can't get back to sleep—you'll find them wide awake with you, cursing the dark, making you laugh, and maybe even soothing you back to slumber. Or let these poems rile you into righteous action, whether it's "leaning in" harder or letting go sooner—whatever moves you toward living life on your own terms.

Ultimately, that's what this book is about—crafting a life that you choose, despite the challenges of midlife and beyond. As we grow older in a culture of constant self-scrutiny and social snark, let's destigmatize aging by talking about it (and living it) without embarrassment and dread, without shame or self-loathing. Let's build on a moment when attitudes toward "aging while female" just may be changing: from Beyoncé to the Notorious RBG (Ruth Bader Ginsburg), Amanda Peet to Ava DuVernay, Emma Watson to Emma Thompson, Shonda Rhimes to Sonia Sotomayor...to Oprah and beyond (we can hardly stop ourselves)—smart, powerful women are already rejecting and subverting cultural norms around growing up and growing older.

We want to join our voices with theirs, and add the resonance of poetry, which endures when trends have come and gone. Great poetry—funny and tender, piercing and true—can help us face both the insults to the flesh and the injuries to the soul that come with growing older. As we've done for each other, we'll accompany you through it all, from a state of shock and frustration to a feeling of peace and acceptance, as in Grace Paley's "Here":

*Here I am in the garden laughing*
*an old woman with heavy breasts*
*and a nicely mapped face.*

*how did this happen*
*well that's who I wanted to be*

Age is coming for us all, but we will be who we want to be, and poetry can help us see and remember that. Amid all the craziness of our lives, poetry offers what Robert Frost called "a momentary stay against confusion"; it cuts through the noise and stays with you, so that no matter the "how did this happen?" moment, you feel grounded, supported, not alone.

Poet Jane Hirshfield says it best:

*Poems are turned to in the great transition of a life, when we are at sea amid changes too vast to feel in any way the master of. One of the things poems do is demonstrate that you aren't alone— that other human beings have been here before, and have found a way to sustain aliveness, to find beauty within the conditions of grief. And this allows you to go on.*

Someday Taylor Swift and her squad will see that first gray hair or have that scare at the ob-gyn, and then they, too, like millions of the rest of us, will feel better thanks to poems like Margaret Atwood's "Solstice Poem, iv":

*My daughter crackles paper, blows
on the tree to make it live, festoons
herself with silver.*

*So far she has no use*
*for gifts.*

*What can I give her,*
*what armor, invincible*
*sword or magic trick, when that year comes?*

*How can I teach her*
*some way of being human*
*that won't destroy her?*

*I would like to tell her, Love*
*is enough, I would like to say,*
*Find shelter in another skin.*

*I would like to say, Dance*
*and be happy. Instead I will say*
*in my crone's voice, Be*
*ruthless when you have to, tell*
*the truth when you can,*
*when you can see it.*

*Iron talismans, and ugly, but*
*more loyal than mirrors.*

# Insult

(WHEN YOU DON'T
RECOGNIZE YOURSELF
IN THE MIRROR)

*It's so funny because it doesn't matter what you do . . . there are days where you're just feeling it and other days where you look at yourself and say, "Oh my god, who is that old woman in the store window? Oh my god, it's me!"*

—AMY POEHLER

Mary never thought she'd care about "growing old." Through her twenties and thirties she worked out, ate right, slept decently. Surely staying healthy and fit would carry her through, and the rest was vanity. A few wrinkles, meh, no big deal. What mattered was doing good work, changing the world, being kind.

Then one day, somewhere around age forty-two,

she happened to touch her chin. What the—she went to the mirror—was that a hair? A spiky black hair growing out of her chin? Repelled but fascinated, she flicked it with her thumb and watched it spring back, perky, pointy, and smug.

En garde. Game on. "Old" was coming for her, one hormonal jab at a time, and what was she going to do about it?

But wait a minute, this couldn't be. Mary had just gotten married at thirty-nine, had a baby at forty-one. Couldn't she rest on this Desitin-stained plateau for a while? Wasn't it enough to be slack bellied and sleep deprived, trying to maintain some semblance of a career? Did this growing-old stuff have to start now, too?

Let's face it: most of us think we're fine with "aging," until some random, superficial thing freaks us out. Separately, you can handle each little insult: pluck the rude hair, hide the gray, pretend your yoga pants are office appropriate. But collectively, these physical changes take a toll on your psyche. You feel the shock—a glancing blow, at first—of not quite looking like you any longer, the sting of realizing others see you differently now, too.

It's a sneak attack, this aging thing, and that's what these first poems are all about—that dawning awareness and disbelief, that prickle of fear, those creeping indignities you try to ignore.

And why should we care about the cosmetic changes of aging? Women should be able to look how they look at any age. Our choice, our identity, our power. Right? If only. Instead, as Sarah Silverman reveals in her tweet turned poem "42 AND Female," we're expected to apologize for daring to be women who (gasp) grow older. Horrifying! Look away!

Okay, so it's a sexist culture, and as Toni Morrison says, physical beauty is one of the "most destructive ideas in the history of human thought." We know we should reject the demand to "age pretty." Let's age smart and strong! We're full-grown women, dammit. Why, oh why, then, do we fret over crow's-feet and muffin tops? Why that trickle of cold sweat when we realize our bodies really are changing all over again, seemingly beyond our control?

Perhaps because there's comfort and familiarity in our "same as I've always looked" youngish selves. We survived the natural disasters of puberty and the bad haircuts of our twenties. Finally we're at home in our skin and confident out in the world—until suddenly we find ourselves, like the speaker in Ariwara No Narihira's "That It Is a Road," going down a road we "never expected" to take so soon.

Even if we strive to be as proudly defiant as Sarah Silverman, the truth is, deep down we feel a bit sad, a bit confused, and a bit embarrassed to admit it. Women often don't talk to one another about these feelings, and there's no *What to Expect When You're Not Really Expecting to Get Older (But Then It Happens Anyway)*.

Too often we're stuck in our own heads, noticing little signs of decrepitude and quietly panicking, like the woman in Deborah Landau's "Solitaire," for whom a summer trip to the pool becomes a frantic meditation on mortality. It's only the "midsummer" of her life, she tells herself. She's not yet "on the oxygen tank." She still has sex twice a week. (You know you're getting older when sex becomes just another item on a list proving you're not yet dead.)

But as she watches the "lithe girls poolside,"

the woman's fears unspool: she wants to "hold on awhile," if she can only figure out how: "If I retinol. If I marathon. / If I Vitamin C. If I crimson // my lips and streakish my hair. / If I wax. Exfoliate. Copulate." But it's too late, she knows. All the cosmetic fixes in the world won't save her from the catastrophes she sees lying in wait: "If a tremor, menopause. Cancer. ALS. / These are the ABCs of my fear."

Exactly. With that first shock of recognition—wow, I look just like the frowzy old moms I used to see at the pool when I was a teenager—comes a cold stab of "oh my god, THIS is how it happens, and what house of horrors lies ahead?"

We feel those moments early in our awareness of aging, but then somehow we recover, repress our dread, and move on in the "tumble-rush of days we cannot catch." The shock of aging recedes until the next little reminder kicks us in the gut, as in Faith Shearin's "Being Called Ma'am." The woman in the poem feels good at forty ("Don't my jeans still fit? Can't I see / without glasses if I just hold the book a little farther // from my face?"), until the college boys with "faces like unused maps" call her ma'am, "that word their mothers taught them." Suddenly she sees the distance between "the woman they see and the one / of my imagination." Suddenly she feels "sexless" and "heavy as silence."

Undeniably, this hurts, when we start to feel unseen, undesirable, unheard. At first it's just a curious observation. In our minds we're still just our lovable selves, looking out at the world through the same eyes we've always had, expecting, perhaps, the same glances we used to get, the same frisson of potential attraction—or at least just friendly recognition. We make eye contact, smile, and . . . the other person walks right by. Ouch. What's going on here? Have we lost our currency—society values youthful beauty (especially in women)—already? Yes, banish the thought—it's unfeminist and offensive, but come on, how many women have thought it, with a mixture of rueful embarrassment and righteous indignation?

There's no getting around the societal truth that as women grow older, everything around sex starts to get a little weird (as if it's all made such great sense before). We may start to question our own desirability, feeling insecure and resentful at the same time. We may start to notice our own sleepy libido, like the speaker in Chana Bloch's very funny "Tired Sex," who catches herself "yawning" during the act, likening herself to "the sparrow the cat / keeps batting around." Sex can be great as we age, sure, yeah, absolutely... and at times it can be just one more thing to do before sorting the laundry. But we can't let it lapse, can't stop initiating, participating in, and (we can't believe we're even saying this), actually enjoying it because then it might be true—maybe we really are sexless ghosts, the "ma'ams" of the world. So we keep the pressure on ourselves to look and feel "sexy," and god forbid we talk about any of it unless we're just joking around.

It is easier, after all, to speak playfully about our changing selves than to reveal the dark abyss of our worry. Tina Fey cracks us up with her *Bossypants* description of "aging naturally":

> *At a certain point, your body wants to be disgusting. While your teens and twenties were about identifying and emphasizing your "best features," your late thirties and forties are about fighting back decay. You pluck your patchy beard daily.*

*Your big toe may start to turn jauntily inward. Overnight you may grow one long, straight white pubic hair.*

And Samantha Bee admits, "I'd prefer to stay 43 forever—but that's not likely to happen. Things are going to sag, things are going to get crepey, some of us (I'm not saying who) are going to grow mysterious catlike whiskers out of weird places (deal with it)." Like them, the woman in Jennifer Tonge's "Self-Portrait at 38" tries to keep things light and funny as she observes her not-exactly-a-work-of-art body.

Sylvia Plath, on the other hand, scares us straight to the Botox doc with her poem about a mirror who lords his power over an aging woman. "I am not cruel, only truthful," the mirror purrs as he delivers his devastating critique of her appearance:

*Each morning it is her face that replaces the darkness.*
*In me she has drowned a young girl, and in me an old woman*
*Rises toward her day after day, like a terrible fish.*

Ultimately, *this* is the fight we need to take to the streets. We can't let our mirrors, literal or figurative—ourselves, our inner judge, our smartphones—tell us we're revolting for showing COMPLETELY NORMAL HUMAN signs of aging. Remember when we felt like "terrible fish" or worse, back when we began sprouting breasts and pubic hair and pimples? The horror-show absurdity of bleeding every month? Wasn't that other, completely normal stage of aging enough weirdness and shame for one life cycle?

And yes, our idiot culture takes the blame for thoroughly indoctrinating us in sexist propaganda where no beautiful woman ages past, say, twenty-one. But bemoaning our "old woman" faces and "surreal" bodies just gives more power to that very culture; worse, we participate in passing it on to the next generation. Even the twenty-two-year-old speaker in Natalie Wise's "Tell Us a Story, Grandma" is already nostalgic for her youth, imagining what wisdom she'll pass on to her grandchildren, feeling old before her time.

That's another shock of aging—you hear yourself complaining about "young people," like some clichéd old codger. Those young people with their slang and fashion and just cool, stimulating, beautiful everything that used to flow through your veins, too. Now you resent and envy them at the same time, like the speaker in Roddy Lumsden's hilarious, poignant "The Young." "You bastards!" he cries. With "sprites in your bones and spite not yet / swollen, not yet set," the young "gather handful / after miracle handful."

Yes, beautiful, lucky youth, and stupid, clunky age—why one following the other, why now, why ever? We're allowed sometimes to throw a massive temper tantrum about it, like Euripides' Herakles: "Age is miserable, tainted with death; / I hate it. Away with it, let the sea swallow it!" Or we can strive for the maturity of the thirty-five-year-old mother in Sharon Olds' "35/10." While brushing her ten-year-old daughter's hair, the mom notices "the grey gleaming" on her own head, and wonders:

> *. . . Why is it*
> *just as we begin to go*
> *they begin to arrive, the fold in my neck*
> *clarifying as the fine bones of her*
> *hips sharpen?*

But if we're brave enough to ask the questions, we also need grace enough to accept the answers. Why the insults and absurdities of "growing older" just as we're coming into our own? Why do we feel so shocked, ever so slightly betrayed? Because, as the mother realizes, "It's an old / story—the oldest we have on our planet— / the story of replacement." And we just aren't ready to be replaced. We want too much still, and maybe always will.

We glimpse the gray and the gross of encroaching age; we feel the chill of A.E. Housman's "Into my heart an air that kills," but the poems in this section help us deflect these early slights, acknowledge the little changes, and push past the discomfort. There's relief in knowing others have been where you are, especially if you've been holding inside all your secret little twinges of "oh my god, is this normal aging stuff or am I dying or am I hideous and what's everyone else doing about this and what should I do?"

Besides, there's mordant comfort in Emily Dickinson's clear-eyed observation about the difference between fear and despair: it's like the difference between the "instant of a Wreck," and "when the

Wreck has been." Huge difference. In one, you see it coming, and in the other, well, we'll get to that stage later.

For now, you're not a Wreck. Just a person getting ever so slightly, normally, humanly older. We're right there with you.

# 42 AND Female

### *(A found poem discovered in a Sarah Silverman tweet)*

Oh my gosh I'm embarrassed. i just found out
I'm a woman AND I'm 42. I am so sorry

@SARAHKSILVERMAN 12:12 AM—6 SEP 2013

# That It Is a Road

That it is a road
Which someday we all travel
I had heard before,
Yet I never expected
To take it so soon myself.

—ARIWARA NO NARIHIRA

# Solitaire

That summer there was no girl left in me.
It gradually became clear.
It suddenly became.

In the pool, I was more heavy than light.
Pockmarked and flabby in a floppy hat.
What will my body be

when parked all night in the earth?
Midsummer. Breathe in. Breathe out.
I am not on the oxygen tank.

Twice a week we have sex.
The lithe girls poolside I see them
at their weddings I see them with babies their hips

thickening I see them middle-aged.
I can't see past the point where I am.
Like you, I'm just passing through.

I want to hold on awhile.
Don't want to naught
or forsake, don't want

to be laid gently or racked raw.
If I retinol. If I marathon.
If I Vitamin C. If I crimson

my lips and streakish my hair.
If I wax. Exfoliate. Copulate
beside the fish-slicked sea.

Fill me I'm cold. Fill me I'm halfway gone.
Would you crush me in the stairwell?
Could we just lie down?

If the brakes don't work.
If the pesticides won't wash off.
If the seventh floor pushes a brick

out the window and it lands on my head.
If a tremor, menopause. Cancer. ALS.
These are the ABCs of my fear.

The doctor says
*I don't have a pill for that, dear.*
Well, what would be a cure-all, ladies,

gin-and-tonics on a summer night?
See you in the immortalities! O blurred.
O tumble-rush of days we cannot catch.

—DEBORAH LANDAU

# Being Called Ma'am

The summer I turn forty I pretend I am still young
      enough
to sit with my college self at the library before
      disappearing

in a field of smoke. Don't my jeans still fit?
      Can't I see
without glasses if I just hold the book a little
      farther

from my face? Then, hiking with my daughter,
      I find
myself talking to a group of college boys, the sort

I would have gone camping with twenty
      years before,
their faces like unused maps. And when they
      answer

they call me ma'am, that word their mothers taught
        them,
or some old schoolmarm maybe, demanding
        respect.

A distance opens between the woman they see and
        the one
of my imagination and I am not someone they
        might laugh with

in the library but instead the stern face that
        appears from
behind the stacks to remind them of their
        manners.

I am the finger over the lips: sexless, as heavy as
        silence.

—FAITH SHEARIN

# Tired Sex

Trying to strike a match in a matchbook
that has lain all winter under the woodpile:
damp sulphur
on sodden cardboard.
I catch myself yawning. Through the window
I watch the sparrow the cat
keeps batting around.

Like turning the pages of a book the teacher
            assigned—

You ought to read it, she said.
It's great literature.

—CHANA BLOCH

# Self-Portrait at 38

Hair still Titian,
but Botticelli's grip has loosened—

not now Rubenesque,
and probably never;

Ingres approaches,
But Courbet might capture me.

Could I be surreal?
It seems almost likely—

bells in my ears
and fortresses under;

cones have been set on my eyes.
My spring is gone

and summer's upon me,
rude in its ripening.

I'm espaliered, strung wide and tied,
Pinioned, and thus can I fly.

—JENNIFER TONGE

# Mirror

I am silver and exact. I have no preconceptions.
What ever you see I swallow immediately
Just as it is, unmisted by love or dislike.
I am not cruel, only truthful—
The eye of a little god, four-cornered.
Most of the time I meditate on the opposite wall.
It is pink, with speckles. I have looked at it so long
I think it is a part of my heart. But it flickers.
Faces and darkness separate us over and over.

Now I am a lake. A woman bends over me,
Searching my reaches for what she really is.
Then she turns to those liars, the candles or the
       moon.
I see her back, and reflect it faithfully.

She rewards me with tears and an agitation of
      hands.
I am important to her. She comes and goes.
Each morning it is her face that replaces the
      darkness.
In me she has drowned a young girl, and in me an
      old woman
Rises toward her day after day, like a terrible fish.

—SYLVIA PLATH

# Tell Us a Story, Grandma

I wonder which ones I will remember:
That I loved my boyfriend's best friend?
That I rode the lonely train to Boston?
That I could never hold myself together?
Maybe I should just tell them
Milk was $2.89 a gallon and bread was $3.29
And an iPhone was $2000
In 2010, when I was 22.

—NATALIE WISE

# The Young

You bastards! It's all sherbet, and folly
makes you laugh like mules. Chances
dance off your wrists, each day ready,

sprites in your bones and spite not yet
swollen, not yet set. You gather handful
after miracle handful, seeing straight,

reaching the lighthouse in record time,
pockets brim with scimitar things. Now
is not a pinpoint but a sprawling realm.

Bewilderment and thrill are whip-quick
twins, carried on your backs, each vow
new to touch and each mistake a broken

biscuit. I was you. Sea robber boarding
the won galleon. Roaring trees. Machines
without levers, easy in bowel and lung.

One cartwheel over the quicksand curve
of Tuesday to Tuesday and you're gone,
summering, a ship on the farthest wave.

—RODDY LUMSDEN

# From *Herakles*

Youth is what I love
Age weighs on my head like a burden
Heavier than the rock of Etna
It draws a curtain of darkness before my eyes.
Not the wealth of an Eastern throne,
Not a palace of gold
Would I take in exchange for youth.
Youth is most precious in prosperity,
Most precious in poverty;
Age is miserable, tainted with death;
I hate it. Away with it, let the sea swallow it!
Why must the curse of age fall on men's homes and
        cities?
Away to the winds with it!

—EURIPIDES

# 35/10

Brushing out our daughter's brown
silken hair before the mirror
I see the grey gleaming on my head,
the silver-haired servant behind her. Why is it
just as we begin to go
they begin to arrive, the fold in my neck
clarifying as the fine bones of her
hips sharpen? As my skin shows
its dry pitting, she opens like a moist
precise flower on the tip of a cactus;
as my last chances to bear a child
are falling through my body, the duds among them,
her full purse of eggs, round and
firm as hard-boiled yolks, is about
to snap its clasp. I brush her tangled
fragrant hair at bedtime. It's an old
story—the oldest we have on our planet—
the story of replacement.

—SHARON OLDS

# Into my heart an air that kills

Into my heart an air that kills
From yon far country blows:
What are those blue remembered hills,
What spires, what farms are those?

That is the land of lost content,
I see it shining plain,
The happy highways where I went
And cannot come again.

—A.E. HOUSMAN

# The difference between Despair

The difference between Despair
And Fear—is like the One
Between the instant of a Wreck
And when the Wreck has been—

The Mind is smooth—no Motion—
Contented as the Eye
Upon the Forehead of a Bust—
That knows—it cannot see—

—EMILY DICKINSON

# Injury

## (WHEN YOU REALIZE AGING IS A THING)

*So. Yes. We're all dying. We're all crumbling
into the void, one cell at a time. We are
disintegrating like sugar cubes in champagne.*

—CAITLIN MORAN

*Anything you think is wrong with your body at
the age of thirty-five you will be nostalgic for at
the age of forty-five.*

—NORA EPHRON

*How has she become one of those people who
wears yoga pants all day? She used to make
fun of those people. With their happiness
maps and their gratitude journals and their*

> *bags made out of recycled tire treads. But now it seems possible that the truth about getting older is that there are fewer and fewer things to make fun of until finally there is nothing you are sure you will never be.*
>
> —JENNY OFFILL

Excellent, you've survived the first jolts of "oh my god I'm getting old." That was unpleasant, but you've got this now. A few physical adjustments (hello, Spanx and SPF 30), a little spiritual soothing (SoulCycle on Sundays), and you're good to go again.

Because forty is the new twenty, and gray is the new green, and you're going to crush this aging thing. Besides, you're too busy busy busy to bother with—holy god, your foot hurts. What's up with that? Plantar fascia-whatsits? Orthopedic inserts, are you kidding? Wait, when did that small print get so blurry? No, your back can't go out, you do Pilates! Dense breast tissue? Basal cell carcinoma? Gum recession? TMJ?

If Insult is all about the shock of aging, Injury is all

about physical deterioration. What seemed relatively skin-deep you now feel in your very bones, muscles, and organs you never wanted to think about. In Mary's midforties all kinds of stuff started conking out in completely unexpected ways, and as soon as she chased down one thing (a numb blue-and-white finger? Raynaud's syndrome!), something else bizarre popped up (no central vision in one eye? Central serous retinopathy!). And forget periods: one month, nothing; the next, a *Game of Thrones* bloodbath.

Mary had no patience for it, none. When her laptop so much as flickers, she's on the phone with Apple Support, politely demanding that the nice people there take care of it ASAP, so she can get on with her life. But her body glitching out, without a warranty? Where was her direct line to 1-800-FIX-THIS?

No, when our bodies start revealing their expiration dates, all we have is the near silence Adelaide Crapsey describes in "November Night":

*With faint dry sound,*
*Like steps of passing ghosts,*
*The leaves, frost-crisp-d, break from the trees*
*And fall.*

Sure, you go to the doctor for your random afflictions, but you feel oddly embarrassed or somehow to blame for things falling apart. You hide your angst from family and friends, thinking, who really wants to hear about this?

We don't want you to feel that eerie quiet when things go weird with your body and your worry makes you feel like a "frost-crisp-d" leaf succumbing to the gravitational pull of "aging." You aren't a "passing ghost" going through this on your own; you're just like the rest of us. Now, if only the rest of us would actually talk about it.

Lucky for all of us, the poems in this section put it all out there: the way injuries and ailments start to mess with our lives (not just our egos), but also the way we can laugh, wince, and slog our way through it, together. These poems will do for you what Elizabeth did for Mary, and what Virginia Woolf said we all need to do for each other: tell the truth about our "experiences as a body." (Seventeen years Mary's senior, Elizabeth regaled her with the details of "hemorrhaging blood" when menopausal and getting gum grafts at age fifty, warning Mary to "floss those teeth now, honey.")

See, for starters, we just uttered the "m" word—
the kiss of death, literally, for our ovaries, and meta-
phorically for anyone hoping to keep an audience
listening. The "m" word, like Voldemort, Shall
Not Be Named. So let's just go ahead and shout it,
get it out of the way, as a middle-aged Hermione
might do (much to Ron's chagrin, no doubt): MENO-
PAUSE. Yeah, that happens, our hormones bounc-
ing around pre-, peri-, and post-, wreaking havoc
on our sleep, body temperature, and mood. As the
speaker in Moira Egan's "What the Flesh Is Heir
To" says:

> *Our mothers never told us there'd be days*
> *(and weeks and months and years) like this; you think*
> *they took a vow of silence? Anyway,*
> *I think somebody needs to make a kit*
> *like the one they gave out in sixth grade,*
> *the pads and belts,* Something Happens to Girls:
> *it's normal, said the booklet, don't be afraid.*

It's normal, yes, but it's also unfamiliar, confus-
ing, and uncomfortable. There's the slightly foggy
brain, the forgetting of little things—your keys,

your phone, the name of that guy who sings that song that's on the tip of your tongue—as in William Butler Yeats' "The Balloon of the Mind."

Then there's the terrible insomnia that assaults you night after night, exquisitely captured by Gerard Manley Hopkins in "I wake and feel the fell of dark, not day": "What hours, O what black hours we have spent / This night!," as if the speaker, too, has lived through those two a.m. wake-ups, heart pounding, mind racing, too hot and then too cold. "The lost are like this," he says, "and their scourge to be / As I am mine, their sweating selves; but worse."

Yes, their sweating selves we are, particularly when hot flashes accompany the night waking; then indeed "I am gall, I am heartburn," as Hopkins says. Mary used to think it was funny when Elizabeth would suddenly start fanning herself—ha-ha, she was such a comedienne when she carried on about these "old lady" things. It was utterly foreign to Mary, but endearing, like the cigarettes Elizabeth chain-smoked and the way she loved Elvis. But now, oh now, Mary knows, like the speaker in Moira Egan's "Not Flashing but Waving," that "clement

flash of heat," that "surge / magmatic, elemental."
She knows what it's like to feel suddenly, helplessly
"Red in visage / and hot as Hades." To be clear: it
sucks.

As does that first mammogram. And the second
one they call you back for because they think they
see something in the first. Sitting in those waiting
rooms feeling cold sweat slide down to your elbows,
imagining the new woman your husband will marry
once you're gone, your son growing up without you.
Thinking of everyone you've ever known who has
faced cancer, trying to be polite to the technicians
as they squoosh your breast into their contraptions.
And then—cascading relief, if you're lucky enough
to hear "benign," like the speaker in Jo McDougall's
"Mammogram":

> *I suddenly love*
> *the radiologist, the nurse, my paper gown,*
> *the vapid print on the dressing room wall.*

Elated by her reprieve, the woman pulls on her
"radiant clothes" and steps into the parking lot as if
it's one of the Seven Wonders of the World.

Who knew midlife meant a new round of standardized tests designed to terrify you about your future? Blood pressure and cholesterol, blood sugar and bone density, MRIs and CT scans. So many parts of the body, so many specialists, so many times the body "wakens from the dream of health" to "hands impersonal as wax," as in Linda Pastan's "At the Gynecologist's." And, always looming, the colonoscopy. Good god, the colonoscopy, that exercise in humility, as described in Eric Rawson's rawly funny "At Fifty." (Yes, there's nothing like a "scope up your ass" to remind you once and for all that "from now on you're something between salvage / and experiment. Everything hurts. / You bleed a little. It's a kind of test.")

Just remember, this stuff is scary but manageable (you hope). You can get through it. (Right?)

Think about all the stupid things you did in adolescence, that other "change of life," and somehow, miraculously, here you are—it's just that back then you didn't think about your vulnerable body, the lack of control, the gazillion ways you and those you love could be taken down. No, you just hopped in cars with really drunk people behind the wheel and hoped your hair still looked good when you got to the next party. Now you are the person behind the wheel, sober, ideally, headed to playdates or meetings, vacations and reunions. Now there's so much at stake... and so much anxiety.

"But we are only in the middle, / only mid-way," cries the woman in Deborah Landau's "Minutes, Years." And she's right. We have families, thriving(ish) careers, burgeoning adult lives—how can it be that our organs are "growing older in their plush pockets / ticking toward the wearing out"? Look at all the homey things that must mean that we're safe for now: "the cozy bed stuffed dog pillows books clock." Why, then, this "pressure in the chest," this nervous checking to make sure not only that we are okay but that those we love are still "breathing / for now, in and out, all night"?

Because with each weird period or herniated disc or abnormal test result we finally get it: growing older means growing OLD. "I am twenty. I am thirty. I am forty years old," chokes the woman, adding, "A friend said *Listen, / you have to try to calm down*."

Right, calming down, perhaps the toughest "test" of aging at this stage. We can tell ourselves that growing older isn't just about loss; it's about expansion, wisdom, opportunity—but then late at night, wide-awake once again, we're worrying about our aging parents, or bargaining with the gods for our partners and kids, as in Deborah Garrison's "A Human Calculation." Like the parent in Devin Johnston's "Fixed Interval," we ultimately face the "plain arithmetic" of our limited time: "When he turns fifteen, you'll be fifty-four. / When he turns thirty, / you'll be sixty-nine / . . . When he turns sixty you'll be gone. / Compacted mud, annealed by summer heat."

So what to do? We can run away and fake being brave, like the woman in Gail Mazur's "Why You Travel." "You don't sit / in a stiff chair and worry, you keep moving," posting photos of yourself "at the Buddhist caves" or "on the Great Wall"—even though deep down "the acid of your fear could eat the world." Or we can attempt to turn inward and hope for a mind-body miracle, like the wife in Jenny Offill's *Dept. of Speculation* (one of our favorite novels):

> *People keep telling me to do yoga. I tried it once at the place down the street. The only part I liked was that part at the end when the teacher covered*

*you with a blanket and you got to pretend you were*
*dead for ten minutes.*

We can obsess over every ache, bulge, and diag-
nosis, until we see ourselves as nothing but hideous
caricatures of our once young selves, deserving
objects of Horace's sexist scorn ("The sweat and
nasty smell get worse all over / her wrinkled body,
as my penis droops / and raging passion cools")
and Villon's misogynistic disdain ("The breasts?
Shrunk again. / The buttocks gone the way of the
tits."). No, guys, tell us how you *really* feel.

Another option. We can strive for a little per-
spective and compassion, not the easiest thing in a
culture that Photoshops the realities of aging. Crack
a gentle joke at your own expense if you like, for
starters, like Dame Judi Dench: "Someone said to
me, 'You have such a wealth of knowledge,' and I
just said, 'I'd rather be young and know nothing,
actually.' Bugger the wealth of knowledge."

Maybe reacquaint yourself with that "Last Fuck-
able Day" sketch (clearly, we're obsessed), to see
strong women eviscerate the absurdity of "aging while
female," while encouraging us to reclaim our worth

as normal, complex, promising women. And while you're at it, read, celebrate, and find inspiration in the work of game-changing women all around you (from Melinda Gates to your mom), kick-ass women who won't take no for an answer when faced with physical or cultural limitations of "growing older." They push back creatively. They hold a mirror up to us collectively as women and reveal the glory of our "pied beauty": "All things counter, original, spare, strange; / Whatever is fickle, freckled (who knows how?) / With swift, slow; sweet, sour; adazzle, dim."

Get excited about actually *still being alive*, even if you're a hobbled, menopausal insomniac. Like maybe one more *Gilmore Girls* revival. A new Lin-Manuel Miranda musical. Or the chance, quite seriously, to change the world for the better, as poet Warsan Shire calls us to do in this passage from "what they did yesterday afternoon":

> *later that night*
> *i held an atlas in my lap*
> *ran my fingers across the whole world*
> *and whispered*
> where does it hurt?

*it answered*
everywhere
everywhere
everywhere.


We can allow ourselves to feel the fear and loath-
ing of our increasingly vulnerable bodies—accept
that it is understandable, normal—and then move
out of it together, through poetry, humor, mean-
ingful work, and real, shared knowledge of what it
physically means to age. As M.F.K. Fisher tells us
in *Sister Age*:

> *The Aging Process is a part of most of our lives,*
> *and it remains one we try to ignore until it seems*
> *to pounce upon us. We evade all its signals. We stay*
> *blandly unprepared for some of its obnoxious effects,*
> *even though we have coped with the cracked voices*
> *and puzzling glands of our emerging natures...*
>
> *Parts of the Aging Process are scary, of course, but*
> *the more we know about them, the less they need*
> *be. That is why I wish we were more deliberately*
> *taught, in early years, to prepare for this condition.*

So find a great doctor and ask blunt questions at your checkups; drop the embarrassment. Talk with women older and younger than you, about what to expect in your forties, fifties, and beyond, and how to cope. Oh, and: don't forget to floss.

We can't tell you everything is going to be all right—that there will be no dire diagnoses, no tough nights or months—but we can tell you this is a journey we all face. Yes, again with the cliché, but as the ever-tough Emily Dickinson points out, it takes courage to sail "Down Time's quaint stream / Without an oar," which is pretty much what we're doing in midlife. We don't know quite where our Port is, nor when a Gale will strike. But there's something empowering about seeing ourselves as "Skippers" or "Buccaneers" taking the risk of forging ahead "without a surety from the Wind / Or schedule of the Tide."

Take that, Horace and Villon: we're swashbuckling buccaneers, a little banged up but alive to fight another day. Bring on the Gale!

# November Night

Listen...

With faint dry sound,
Like steps of passing ghosts,
The leaves, frost-crisp-d, break from the trees
And fall.

—ADELAIDE CRAPSEY

# What the Flesh Is Heir To

Our mothers never told us there'd be days
(and weeks and months and years) like this;
      you think
they took a vow of silence? Anyway,
I think somebody needs to make a kit
like the one they gave out in sixth grade,
the pads and belts, *Something Happens to Girls*:
it's normal, said the booklet, don't be afraid.
I need a book like that, with homey pearls
of woman wisdom for this later stage.

Dear Kimberly-Clark:
              We have some suggestions.
We need Kleenex, Lightdays, and also sage
advice about the menopausal question:
To HRT or not.     Soy? Calcium?
And could you please throw in some Halcion?

                        —MOIRA EGAN

# The Balloon of the Mind

Hands, do what you're bid:
Bring the balloon of the mind
That bellies and drags in the wind
Into its narrow shed.

—WILLIAM BUTLER YEATS

# I wake and feel the fell of dark, not day

I wake and feel the fell of dark, not day.
What hours, O what black hours we have spent
This night! what sights you, heart, saw; ways
      you went!
And more must, in yet longer light's delay.
With witness I speak this. But where I say
Hours I mean years, mean life. And my lament
Is cries countless, cries like dead letters sent
To dearest him that lives alas! away.

I am gall, I am heartburn. God's most deep decree
Bitter would have me taste: my taste was me;
Bones built in me, flesh filled, blood brimmed
      the curse.

Selfyeast of spirit a dull dough sours. I see
The lost are like this, and their scourge to be
As I am mine, their sweating selves; but worse.

        —GERARD MANLEY HOPKINS

# Not Flashing but Waving

My poet girlfriend says she asked her Doc
when these things stop. Her Doc said, *Maybe never.*
Dear God, now I've become a walking, talk-
ing punchline: *Do you think I have a fever?*
or *Is it hot in here, or is it me?*

And worse, why don't they tell us it gets worse?
What used to be a clement flash of heat
has lately metamorphosed to a surge
magmatic, elemental. Red in visage
and hot as Hades, I excuse myself
to douse my head, take marble-cool refuge
in what we euphemize as "room of rest."

And still we euphemize this "moon of pause."
I'm log to flame, I'm fingernails to claws.

—MOIRA EGAN

# Mammogram

"They're benign," the radiologist says,
pointing to specks on the x ray
that look like dust motes
stopped cold in their dance.
His words take my spine like flame.
I suddenly love
the radiologist, the nurse, my paper gown,
the vapid print on the dressing room wall.
I pull on my radiant clothes.
I step out into the Hanging Gardens, the Taj
      Mahal,
the Niagara Falls of the parking lot.

—JO MCDOUGALL

# At the Gynecologist's

The body so carefully
contrived for pain,
wakens from the dream of health
again and again
to hands impersonal as wax
and instruments that pry
into the closed chapters of flesh.
See me here, my naked legs
caught in these metal stirrups,
galloping toward death
with flowers of ether in my hair.

—LINDA PASTAN

# At Fifty

At fifty: they run a scope up your ass
and snip out the precocious pretumors.
You bleed a little. It's a kind of test.

By then you have had minor surgery
on an elbow or eye, and at least one
pharmaceutical dependency to

remind you, having lost your religion,
that the body only barely belongs
to you and is easily corrupted.

You find hard patches and soft patches and
red new patches on your shoulders and scalp.
You can picture your bladder convulsing,

or if you can't, they'll show it on a screen.
The equipment is mostly silent, which
gives a feeling of floating in water.

From now on you're something between salvage
and experiment. Everything hurts.
You bleed a little. It's a kind of test.

—ERIC RAWSON

# Minutes, Years

Before you have kids,
you get a dog.

Then when you get a baby,
you wait for the dog to die.

When the dog dies,
it's a relief.

When your babies aren't babies,
you want a dog again.

The uses of the body,
you see where they end.

But we are only in the middle,
only mid-way.

The organs growing older in their plush pockets
ticking toward the wearing out.

HOW DID THIS HAPPEN?

We are here and soon won't be
(despite the cozy bed stuffed dog pillows books
        clock).

The boy with his socks on and pajamas.
A series of accidental collisions.

Pressure in the chest. Everyone breathing
for now, in and out, all night.

These sad things, they have to be.
I go into the kitchen thinking to sweeten myself.

Boiled eggs won't do a thing.
Oysters. Lysol. Peanut butter. Gin.

Big babyface, getting fed.
I am twenty. I am thirty. I am forty years old.

A friend said *Listen,*
*you have to try to calm down.*

—DEBORAH LANDAU

# A Human Calculation

If it had to be him
or them
let it be him.

If he had to choose between me
and them,
just one of them,
goodbye to me.

Take me.
take him,
God forbid them.

Blasphemous
back of the envelope:
we don't get
to subtract
or make trades.

Only to add
and clutch
at our numbers.

—DEBORAH GARRISON

# Fixed Interval

When he turns fifteen, you'll be fifty-four.
When he turns thirty, you'll be sixty-nine.
This plain arithmetic amazes more
than miracle, the constant difference more
than mere recursion of father in son.
If you reach eighty, he'll be forty-one!

The same sun wheels around again, the dawn
drawn out and hammered thin as a copper sheet.
When he turns sixty you'll be gone.
Compacted mud, annealed by summer heat,
two ruts incise this ghost-forsaken plain
and keep their track width, never to part or meet.

—DEVIN JOHNSTON

# Why You Travel

You don't want the children to know how afraid
you are. You want to be sure their hold on life

is steady, sturdy. Were mothers and fathers
always this anxious, holding the ringing

receiver close to the ear: *Why don't they answer,
where could they be?* There's a conspiracy

to protect the young, so they'll be fearless,
it's why you travel—it's a way of trying

to let go, of lying. You don't sit
in a stiff chair and worry, you keep moving.

Postcards from the Alamo, the Alhambra.
Photos of you in Barcelona, Gaudí's park

swirling behind you. There you are in the Garden
of the master of the Fishing Nets, one red

tree against a white wall, koi swarming
over each other in the thick demoralized pond.

You, fainting at the Buddhist caves.
Climbing with thousands on the Great Wall,

wearing a straw cap, a backpack, a year
before the students at Tiananmen Square.

Having the time of your life, blistered and smiling.
The acid of your fear could eat the world.

—GAIL MAZUR

# From *Epodes*

## VIII

You dare to ask me, you decrepit, stinking slut,
what makes me impotent?
And you with blackened teeth, and so advanced
in age that wrinkles plough your forehead,
your raw and filthy areshole gaping like a cow's
between your wizened buttocks.
It's your slack breasts that rouse me (I have seen
much better udders on a mare)
your flabby paunch and scrawny thighs
stuck on your swollen ankles.

## XII

The sweat and nasty smell get worse all over
her wrinkled body, as my penis droops
and raging passion cools
and all the while the powdered chalk
and crocodile-shit dye run on her face as she
     ruts away,
breaking the bed and the canopy over it...

—HORACE

# From *The Testament*

This is what human beauty comes to:
The arms short, the hands shriveled,
The shoulders all hunched up.
The breasts? Shrunk again.
The buttocks gone the way of the tits.
The quim? Aagh! As for the thighs,
They aren't thighs now but sticks
Speckled all over like sausages

—FRANÇOIS VILLON (TRANSLATED
BY GALWAY KINNELL)

# Pied Beauty

Glory be to God for dappled things—
  For skies of couple-colour as a brinded cow;
    For rose-moles all in stipple upon trout that
      swim;
Fresh-firecoal chestnut-falls; finches' wings;
  Landscape plotted and pieced—fold, fallow,
    and plough;
    And áll trádes, their gear and tackle and trim.

All things counter, original, spare, strange;
  Whatever is fickle, freckled (who knows how?)
    With swift, slow; sweet, sour; adazzle, dim;
He fathers-forth whose beauty is past change:
    Praise him.

—GERARD MANLEY HOPKINS

# what they did yesterday afternoon

they set my aunts house on fire

i cried the way women on tv do
folding at the middle
like a five pound note.
i called the boy who use to love me
tried to 'okay' my voice
i said *hello*
he said *warsan, what's wrong, what's happened?*

i've been praying,
and these are what my prayers look like;
*dear god*
*i come from two countries*
*one is thirsty*
*the other is on fire*
*both need water.*

later that night
i held an atlas in my lap
ran my fingers across the whole world
and whispered
*where does it hurt?*

it answered
*everywhere*
*everywhere*
*everywhere.*

—WARSAN SHIRE

# Down Time's quaint stream

Down Time's quaint stream
Without an oar
We are enforced to sail
Our Port a secret
Our Perchance a Gale
What Skipper would
Incur the Risk
What Buccaneer would ride
Without a surety from the Wind
Or schedule of the Tide—

—EMILY DICKINSON

# Defiance

## (WHEN YOU THINK YOU CAN MAKE IT ALL GO AWAY)

*We are on red alert when it comes to how
we are perceiving ourselves as a species.
There's no desire to be an adult. Adulthood
is not a goal. It's not seen as a gift.
Something happened culturally: No
one is supposed to age past 45—sartorially,
cosmetically, attitudinally. Everybody
dresses like a teenager. Everybody dyes
their hair. Everybody is concerned
about a smooth face.*

—FRANCES MCDORMAND

*I don't feel like I have to please anyone. I feel
free. I feel like I'm an adult. I'm grown. I can
do what I want. I can say what I want. I can*

*retire if I want. That's why I've*
*worked hard.*

—BEYONCÉ

*Yeah, f\*ck you, I'm 50. That's what I'm*
*going to say when I turn 50.*

—MADONNA

Swagger. Bravado. Defiance in the face of aging—that's what the poems in this section address. You're ready to fight it all, the insults *and* the injuries of growing older, from the superficial and scary (gray hair, saggy skin, freaky health stuff) to the societal and existential (sexist standards of beauty, utility, and worth). As real-life, grown-ass women, we've earned the right to push back at aging in whatever way we choose; or as Dorothy Parker sweetly explains in "Indian Summer":

*But now I know the things I know,*
*And do the things I do;*

*And if you do not like me so,*
*To hell, my love, with you!*

We love this stage of things, the bitter fun of a fixed fight, the in-your-faceness of it all. Like when midforties Elizabeth used to wear wee little miniskirts with thick tights, and one of our colleagues in the English Department, swathed in some tentlike garment, would raise her eyebrows and say, "My, you're so brave, Elizabeth," meaning, in fact, "You whore, Elizabeth, what do you think you're doing?"

Elizabeth has remained (nonwhorishly) longlegged, lipsticked, and alluring right into her seventies, her professorial brio imbued with ironic wit and a signature tobacco-meets-Chloé scent. Mary, on the other hand, has resisted aging by sticking to the classic *Harriet the Spy* look first debuted at age twelve: sporty bottoms, T-shirt top, hair in a ponytail, sheen of day-old sweat. Long ago Elizabeth warned her, "This fresh-faced thing won't work forever. Sooner or later you're going to need to try a little mascara."

Did Mary listen? No. Does that make her heroically defiant or simply lazy? Unadventurous? Self-defeating? It's hard to say, because "defying aging" takes so many forms, from reactive denial ("Who's old? Not me!") to more thoughtful, deliberate attempts to reshape your life, reset your priorities. Most of us start from a defensive crouch because "aging" strikes like the bully who snickers as you stumble along clueless, a "kick me" sign flapping on your back. But some of us play offense from the get-go, cultivating sunproof skin, gravity-defying bodies, and Zen mind-sets well before the rest of us have experienced our first periods.

We lurch forward and back in Defiance, sometimes flailing angry and spiteful, sometimes standing proud and sure, and the poems in this section reflect that spectrum. Keep in mind that one woman's "growing old" (a nightmare) is another woman's "growing up" (an opportunity). "Defying age" spins us around till we can't quite tell what we're fighting—our bodies, our culture, our upbringing, death—but it feels good to fight something, to exert our will, to feel relevant, rebellious, and at least something like young.

We're both energized and humbled by our grow-
ing age, emboldened to shoot for everything we've
never done, but all too aware of encroaching limita-
tions. Like the speaker in Rainer Maria Rilke's "You
see, I want a lot," we still "want everything: / the
darkness that comes with every infinite fall / and
the shivering blaze of every step up." We want to
"do work and feel thirst," to be needed, to love and
be loved. Rilke's poem gives us permission to pur-
sue all of it, age be damned: "You have not grown
old, and it is not too late," he says, "to dive into
your increasing depths."

So in we dive—straight to the depths of denial,
like the woman in "Gold Lipstick and the End of
Summer." "Who knows what old ladies are?" she
asks, implying she sure as hell doesn't plan on
becoming one. Instead she'll keep dressing and
acting like all the girls she's ever been, from the
"road-stained warrior trucking girls" to the "gin-
gerbread goodie-goodies." This makes a certain
adolescent sense—we don't know how to adjust to
this new "older person" identity, so we stick with
what's worked in the past, when "girlish charm"—
or Riot Grrrlish thunder—helped us get what we

wanted, before "Resting Bitch Face" was a thing. Look young to stay young, we think, swearing we'll never wear Chico's or turn into Jane Hirshfield's "The Bearded Woman."

But at the same time we're conflicted and ticked off. Of course we're not adolescents, but we're not creatures from the crypt either—and yet we're caught in this *Freaky Friday* limbo of adult womanhood. It's not just about looks; it's about who we are—still vibrant, still viable, still "little punk rabbits" of ingenuity. Is it denial to admit we want more than the fatigued wisdom of "old ladies"?

Oh hell no, says the woman in Lucille Clifton's "there is a girl inside." We're done playing Little Red Riding Hood, and we refuse the role of sickly grandmamma, too. No, the girl inside is "randy as a wolf," ferocious with the desire to "break through gray hairs / into blossom," to reveal her fierce vitality till "the woods [are] wild / with the damn wonder of it." Imagine that, a woman over forty or fifty who still feels ravenously alive and is "wild" enough to show it, at work and at play.

And this is where things get a little tricky for women as we get older. We know we're capable, smart, passionate, and maybe even beautiful, in a totally normal over-forty way, but we feel tremendous pressure to remain "attractive" in a totally abnormal under-thirty way. So we "defy" aging by capitulating to sexist cultural norms: hide the gray, tighten the skin, whiten the teeth—oh hell, as Gaius Lucilius says, "with a make-up bill like yours / you'd save money buying a face." And so we do. Buy a face. Some of us. A little Botox, a lot of Restylane, a laser here, a lift there. And we keep it all very quiet, because the only thing worse than the stigma of looking like a hag at forty is the stigma of admitting you've "had work done."

On the one hand, it's outrageous, the money and time spent on distorting our looks into some mask of "youthful beauty." This excerpt from a 2016 *W* magazine article entitled, "Forever 21," leaves us speechless, unless throwing up counts as speech:

*Part of this shift is due to the fact that our culture is allowing women to be sexy and youthful into their 40s, 50s, and 60s without judgment. But, according to Harold Lancer, the Beverly Hills dermatologist who treats Beyoncé and Scarlett*

*Johansson, the seismic change in how women in the spotlight age has less to do with society than it does skincare...*

*"Dakota Fanning was 9 when she first walked into my office," Lancer says. "I make sure my patients of any age understand the value of exercise, avoiding carbohydrates, salt, and dairy. Then I start them on a skincare routine...My clients aren't just in it for a quick fix. They understand that they're starting a cycle of chronic and expensive maintenance. There's no such thing as planting a garden that doesn't need weeding."*

Wait, our faces are gardens we need to plant? At age nine? And props to "our culture" for "allowing" us to be "sexy and youthful" into our "40s, 50s, and 60s without judgment"? Did we say we were speechless? Happily, Amy Poehler is not, as she shows in "Plastic Surgery Haiku" such as these:

*We know it's Botox*
*And not your vegan diet*
*Nice try, Margaret*

*Can I be honest?*
*You look like a lady from*
*The Broadway show* Cats

We laugh, but Poehler is scratching at something deeper and more uncomfortable than just "ha-ha, let's mock women who think self-mutilation makes them look young." Yes, we are outraged by idiotic standards of beauty—but does that make it okay to shame women who choose to adhere to them? We want to condemn the standards, but we wind up like middle-aged Mean Girls, ridiculing women who perhaps feel just as insecure and vulnerable as when they were teenagers.

Oh, the confusion of "aging while female" in a culture where "Much Madness is divinest Sense," and "Much Sense the starkest Madness" (says good old Emily D.). How to defy aging on a personal scale while also fighting the sexist Majority of the world? Here's a radical solution: we could embrace what actor/producer Frances McDormand calls "the gift" of adulthood, and by our example help others do the same. McDormand shows how it's done in "Laugh Lines" (an interview with Katie

Couric that we turned into a poem). When Couric asks if she's ever shocked by her face on-screen, McDormand responds:

> *Oh yeah, it's not like I don't*
> *look at my face and go*
> *whoa, wow, look at that,*
> *what the—*
> *but I also at the same time [pointing to laugh lines]*
> *—that—*
> *that one right there*
> *that one*
> *that's Pedro. That's my son.*
> *Twenty years of going hi!, wow!, or oh my g—*
> *You know, this is the map.*
> *This is the map.*
> *Even that stuff,*
> *this is the road map.*

Sing it, Frances! Who can hear that and not want to age like her, with ruthless honesty and gratitude? We don't have to be plastic, preachy, or pathetic if we make "growing older" about how we *live*—each woman choosing her own way—not how we *look*.

As writer Zadie Smith observes, "Something changes when women are forced out of the beauty industry and the marital fantasy industry—I think they become their real selves. Women…in their fifties…are humans, not refracted images of some insane feminine myth." Exactly. Like Snow White in Anne Sheldon's "Snow White Turns 39," we can smash the "talking mirror" (the endless "who's the fairest of them all?" feed from Hollywood, Facebook, fashion) and "take up chess"—use our minds, develop our talents, reject the "tidy kingdom" that keeps us "under glass." Growing older can become a game of strategy, not surrender, and we can play it like a badass chess queen (the only one free to move any way she likes on the board). Instead of sniping at one another, or feeling alone, we can change the rules of "aging while female," if enough of us stop chasing fairy tales and instead choose "to be of use," as in the first lines of Marge Piercy's poem by that title:

*The people I love the best*
*jump into work head first*
*without dallying in the shallows*
*and swim off with sure strokes almost out of sight.*

Yes, this is how you really defy aging—by finding good work and doing it well. That's how to draft a "road map" like McDormand's. Whether it's for a job, a cause, or a community, get out of your own little life and "move in a common rhythm" with the larger world. When we commit to "work that is real"—a concrete practice that brings joy—we find that "the thing worth doing well done / has a shape that satisfies, clean and evident."

There's a liberating clarity that comes with this kind of defiance: freed from inane expectations, some women set about becoming their best selves at midlife and beyond, leaving toxic jobs and relationships, refining their abilities, and, like the swimmer in Claudia Emerson's "Lifeguard," saving their own lives. So much to love about this poem, including that it's a Defiance counterpoint to Deborah Landau's swimming pool poem in Insult. In Landau's poem, the woman feels self-conscious and vulnerable compared to the "lithe girls poolside." But in Emerson's poem, the roles are reversed, and the teenage girl lifeguard is the one who seems "faded," "dangling," and lost in "shallow dreams," as the middle-aged woman triumphantly swims "length after predictable // length" within the "taut confines / of the brightly buoyed lane." Abandoned by the snoozing lifeguard, the swimmer declares,

> *... I've never felt so safe in my life,*
>
> *making flawless, practiced turns, pushing, invisible*
> *to reenter my own wake, reverse it.*

And this is how we'd like to leave you in Defiance: self-reliant and satisfied, not only pushing against time but almost reversing it.

But it's so bittersweet knowing that Claudia Emerson died of colon cancer at age fifty-seven, two years after "Lifeguard" was published. Through her stunning poems she defies death, yes, but again, we hear Virginia Woolf urging us to tell the truth about the experience of women's bodies. So we end with a piercingly funny, brave poem by Anne Boyer, written as she struggled with breast cancer. Anyone who has been through the absurdity of serious illness will recognize herself in this elegant,

one-sentence rant, a Wile E. Coyote–like medita-
tion that begins:

*Always falling into a hole, then saying, "ok, this is
not your grave, get out of this hole," getting out of
the hole which is not the grave, falling into a hole
again, saying "ok this is also not your grave, get
out of this hole"...*

And in the middle looks like this:

*sometimes falling into holes with other people,
with other people, saying "this is not our mass
grave, get out of this hole," all together getting out
of the hole together, hands and legs and arms and
human ladders of each other to get out of the hole
that is not the mass grave...*

And which ends with this:

*sometimes too ardently contemplating the final
hole while trying to avoid the provisional ones;
sometimes dutifully falling and getting out, with
perfect fortitude, saying "look at the skill and*

*spirit with which I rise from that which resembles
the grave but isn't!"*

And so armed with the plucky fortitude of those
who have risen from that which resembles the grave
but isn't, we head to the darkest section of the book,
Dread, the "final hole" which must be faced if it's to
be overcome, or at least, through great poetry like
Emerson's and Boyer's, defied.

# Indian Summer

In youth, it was a way I had
To do my best to please,
And change, with every passing lad,
To suit his theories.

But now I know the things I know,
And do the things I do;
And if you do not like me so,
To hell, my love, with you!

—DOROTHY PARKER

# You see, I want a lot

You see, I want a lot.
Perhaps I want everything:
the darkness that comes with every infinite fall
and the shivering blaze of every step up.

So many live on and want nothing,
and are raised to the rank of prince
by the slippery ease of their judgments.

But what you love to see are faces
that do work and feel thirst.

You love most of all those who need you
as they need a crowbar or a hoe.

You have not grown old, and it is not too late
to dive into your increasing depths
where life calmly gives out its own secret.

—RAINER MARIA RILKE
(TRANSLATED BY ROBERT BLY)

# Gold Lipstick and the End of Summer

Who knows what old ladies are?
They want their copies back
Some cannot recall past lives
This must be satisfying
I must be lazy
I can barely grow old
I am hiding in the bottom drawer
All my girls are there

Aloha girls
Road-stained warrior trucking girls
Ski holiday village girls
Girls with forks of fat
Saintly girls on rosary hum
Disco marigolds
Gingerbread goodie-goodies
Little punk rabbits.

—MELISSA BRODER

# The Bearded Woman

Each time she noticed,
she had meant
to pluck the three black hairs,
but the days were short;
her fingers touched her chin
then forgot.
thus fatigue grew curling into wisdom.

—JANE HIRSHFIELD

# there is a girl inside

there is a girl inside.
she is randy as a wolf.
she will not walk away
and leave these bones
to an old woman.

she is a green tree
in a forest of kindling.
she is a green girl
in a used poet.

she has waited
patient as a nun
for the second coming,
when she can break through gray hairs
into blossom

and her lovers will harvest
honey and thyme
and the woods will be wild
with the damn wonder of it.

——LUCILLE CLIFTON

# Wig, rouge, honey

Wig, rouge, honey, wax, teeth:
with a make-up bill like yours
you'd save money buying a face.

—GAIUS LUCILIUS (TRANSLATED
BY PETER PORTER)

# Selected "Plastic Surgery Haiku"

We know it's Botox
And not your vegan diet
Nice try, Margaret

Plastic surgery
Requires a good amount
Of lying to friends

Can I be honest?
You look like a lady from
The Broadway show *Cats*

I have no idea
If you are angry or sad
Since you got fillers

Hey, shooting poison
In your face does not keep you
From turning fifty

—FROM *YES PLEASE* BY AMY POEHLER

# Much Madness is divinest Sense

Much Madness is divinest Sense—
To a discerning Eye—
Much Sense—the starkest Madness—
'Tis the Majority
In this, as All, prevail—
Assent—and you are sane—
Demur—you're straightway dangerous—
And handled with a Chain—

—EMILY DICKINSON

# Laugh Lines

*(a found poem discovered in an interview
with Frances McDormand)*

Katie Couric asked Frances McDormand:
*Do you ever have these moments
when you see yourself on screen,
Frances,
and you think,
Gah!*

Oh yeah, it's not like I don't
look at my face and go
whoa, wow, look at that,
what the—
but I also at the same time [pointing to laugh lines]
—that—
that one right there
that one
that's Pedro. That's my son.

Twenty years of going hi!, wow!, or oh my g—
You know, this is the map.
This is the map.
Even that stuff,
this is the road map.

# Snow White Turns 39

I'm planning how to break a talking mirror:
hammer and earplugs. Seven years of bad luck?
Better than that Bette Davis cackle
every morning when I hit the sink
without my make-up. One black dawn, I'll raise
my cheekbones to the light and all those watts
will fail to flush away these tear-track shadows.
Then I will smash the Glass. And take up chess.
No more clipping recipes for sautéed
hearts of virgin, I can tell you that,
or sending milkmaids out to feed the wolves.
No more wolves to feed, or woodsmen, either,
in our tidy kingdom. My husband found me
under glass. How I miss the woodsman.

—ANNE SHELDON

# To be of use

The people I love the best
jump into work head first
without dallying in the shallows
and swim off with sure strokes almost out of sight.
They seem to become natives of that element,
the black sleek heads of seals
bouncing like half-submerged balls.

I love people who harness themselves, an ox to a
        heavy cart,
who pull like water buffalo, with massive patience,
who strain in the mud and the muck to move
        things forward,
who do what has to be done, again and again.

I want to be with people who submerge
in the task, who go into the fields to harvest
and work in a row and pass the bags along,
who are not parlor generals and field deserters

but move in a common rhythm
when the food must come in or the fire be put out.

The work of the world is common as mud.
Botched, it smears the hands, crumbles to dust.
But the thing worth doing well done
has a shape that satisfies, clean and evident.
Greek amphoras for wine or oil,
Hopi vases that held corn, are put in museums
but you know they were made to be used.
The pitcher cries for water to carry
and a person for work that is real.

—MARGE PIERCY

# Lifeguard

She perches high on the stand, gleaming whistle
    dangling, on her suit a dutiful,

faded red cross. Mine her only life
    to guard, she does for a while watch

the middle-aged woman who has nothing better
    to do than swim laps in the Y's indoor pool

on a late Friday afternoon. I am slow,
    though, boring, length after predictable

length of breaststroke or the duller lap
    of elementary backstroke perfectly

executed within the taut confines
    of the brightly buoyed lane. So she abandons me

to study split-ends, hangnail, wristwatch,
    until—the body of the whistle cupped

loosely in her palm—her head nods toward
    shallow dreams. I've never felt so safe in my life,

making flawless, practiced turns, pushing, invisible
    to reenter my own wake, reverse it.

—CLAUDIA EMERSON

# what resembles the grave
# but isn't

Always falling into a hole, then saying "ok, this
is not your grave, get out of this hole," getting
out of the hole which is not the grave, falling into
a hole again, saying "ok, this is also not your
grave, get out of this hole," getting out of that
hole, falling into another one; sometimes falling
into a hole within a hole, or many holes within
holes, getting out of them one after the other,
then falling again, saying "this is not your grave,
get out of the hole"; sometimes being pushed,
saying "you can not push me into this hole, it
is not my grave," and getting out defiantly, then
falling into a hole again without any pushing;
sometimes falling into a set of holes whose
structures are predictable, ideological, and long

dug, often falling into this set of structural and
impersonal holes; sometimes falling into holes
with other people, with other people, saying
"this is not our mass grave, get out of this hole,"
all together getting out of the hole together,
hands and legs and arms and human ladders
of each other to get out of the hole that is not
the mass grave but that will only be gotten out
of together; sometimes the willful-falling into a
hole which is not the grave because it is easier
than not falling into a hole really, but then once
in it, realizing it is not the grave, getting out of
the hole eventually; sometimes falling into a hole
and languishing there for days, weeks, months,
years, because while not the grave very difficult,
still, to climb out of and you know after this
hole there's just another and another; sometimes
surveying the landscape of holes and wishing for
a high quality final hole; sometimes thinking of
who has fallen into holes which are not graves
but might be better if they were; sometimes
too ardently contemplating the final hole while
trying to avoid the provisional ones; sometimes
dutifully falling and getting out, with perfect

fortitude, saying "look at the skill and spirit with which I rise from that which resembles the grave but isn't!"

—ANNE BOYER

# Dread
## (WHEN YOU REALIZE YOU CAN'T EVEN)

*What shall I do with this absurdity—*
*O heart, O troubled heart—this caricature,*
*Decrepit age that has been tied to me*
*As to a dog's tail?*

—WILLIAM BUTLER YEATS

*The problem, unstated till now, is how*
*to live in a damaged body*
*in a world where pain is meant to be gagged*
*uncured    un-grieved-over...*

—ADRIENNE RICH

*And all our yesterdays have lighted fools*
*The way to dusty death.*

—WILLIAM SHAKESPEARE, *MACBETH*

*And so it stays just on the edge of vision,*
*A small unfocused blur, a standing chill*
*That slows each impulse down to indecision.*
*Most things may never happen: this one will,*
*And realisation of it rages out*
*In furnace-fear when we are caught without*
*People or drink.*

—PHILIP LARKIN, "AUBADE"

Terror. Panic. Grief. *Dread.* You can't push it away any longer. Now you're electric with anxiety, not just in the pulsing dark of two a.m., but worse, in the cold sunshine of a perfectly brilliant day.

You managed to cope for a long time, through distraction, denial, and other forms of Defiance—family, work, multitasking, what Landau calls "our habitual flying patterns." But now everything you felt in Injury hits with ten times the force—that sense that anything could happen to you or those you love, any minute, and you're helpless to stop it. Surely it's hormonal, temporary; surely some answer will present itself. But until then you're stuck in this loop of fear, like the woman in Landau's "I Don't Have a Pill for That":

> *The wedding is over.*
> *Summer is over.*
> *Life please explain.*
>
> *This book is nearly halfway read.*
> *I don't have a pill for that,*
> *the doctor said.*

We're scared looking ahead to our future as "old," and we're scared standing still in a vulnerable state of "not quite yet," like a book 'nearly halfway read.'" Now every weird bump and bruise seems fraught with what-ifs, as in Jane Hirshfield's "Bruises." We who used to laugh off our scraped-up, banged-up selves—the carpet burns and graveled knees from younger, sexier days—now find ourselves "kissed by this," this ominous sense of mortality, these symptoms and signs that "have no explanation."

Yes, Life, please explain what's happening at this stage of terror-stricken aging. Unveil the mystery so we can all get on with our lives. The woman gardening in Louise Glück's "Matins" dares God to give her some sign of hope, some cosmic prescription for the panic of summer ending, her life fading. "You want to know how I spend my time?" she cheekily asks God, and then she answers for him:

> I walk the front lawn, pretending
> to be weeding...
> I'm looking for courage, for some evidence
> my life will change...

Here we all are, in this stage of Dread, on our knees (as if in prayer) pretending to weed the clumpy gardens of our lives, even though we're all too aware of

> the leaves turning, always the sick trees
> going first, the dying turning
> brilliant yellow, while a few dark birds perform
> their curfew of music.

How to go on with our daily lives despite the losses of friends and family, despite constant reminders of our own dark curfew? What can we hold on to amid this Dread? Or as the gardening woman asks, "was the point always / to continue without a sign?"

Because here's what we're facing: not just nerves, not just hormones, but a bottomless grief as we lose what we love to unknowable nothingness. "Even now I can't grasp 'nothing' or 'never,'" says the woman in Meghan O'Rourke's "Ever," written after the death of her mother. The words themselves are "unholdable, unglobable, no map to nothing," but the pain is all too palpable: "Never? Never ever again to see you?" Like us, she is caught between rational thought and raw emotion: explain in a way I can understand why this is so hard, God; give us a treatment plan, Doc, because this "guillotine— gutting—never to which we never say goodbye" is too much to take. As the woman concludes, in two lines that gut our hearts:

*Will I ever really get never?*
*You're gone. Nothing, never—ever.*

And here we are, crushed by unfathomable, sorrowful angst like the woman in Kelly Cherry's

"Lines Written on the Eve of a Birthday," who declares, "It is the loss of possibility / That claims you bit by bit."

This is why Dread devastates us: it feels as if everything is taken—pleasures and abilities, old loves and new dreams—in steady, sure fashion, from "the children you had hoped would be" to your "brown hair" replaced by gray.

So perhaps we have a choice here, in the depths of Dread. We can "give up in the end" by making Dread our refuge, by armoring ourselves in bitter anger, as in Margaret Atwood's "Porcupine Meditation." The world is going to hand us unremitting pain and anxiety? Fine, then, we'll settle in, like a porcupine in its den: "head down, spikes out, / brain tucked in." Why bother trying to "outfox" mortality anymore? Why "age pretty," or dream big, or care too much when it will all be snatched away with random cruelty? Instead we will "squat and stink" in dirty sweatpants and a chinful of quills, daring anyone to reach out to us with compassion or comfort:

*Here I am, dogs,*
*nose me over,*

*go away sneezing, snouts full of barbs*
*hooking their way to your brain.*
*Now you've got some*
*of my pain. Much good may it do you.*

That's one route, yes, luxuriating in spite and malice, like the joyless woman in Zhu Shuzhen's "Waking Up." Or giving up altogether, as in Dorothy Parker's "Coda":

*For art is a form of catharsis,*
*And love is a permanent flop,*
*And work is the province of cattle,*
*And rest's for a clam in a shell,*
*So I'm thinking of throwing the battle—*
*Would you kindly direct me to hell?*

And that's fine for a while, to remain inert, paralyzed in the hell of Dread, because in some ways it's easier than trying to live with calm acceptance in a chaotic world. Honestly, who besides Pema, Gwyneth, and Oprah can really achieve that Deepak Chopra Zen?

But what if the way out of Dread—if you want

out, for now, anyway—doesn't mean sedating your-self into some "sweetness and light" version of a "happy older woman," the kind who says things like, "Life over fifty is one never-ending orgasm!" The woman in Lucille Clifton's "it was a dream" shows us a more authentic way forward. Only by facing her disappointments and losses does the woman find her "greater self," who accuses her of wasting her life—but who also shows her what she can do about it:

> *what,*
> *i pleaded with her, could I do,*
> *oh what could I have done?*
> *and she twisted her wild hair*
> *and sparked her wild eyes*
> *and screamed as long as*
> *i could hear her*
> *This. This. This.*

You could regret and mourn "This. This. This." Or you can make something out of "This. This. This." You can write this poem, do this work, reach out to this world, even in all lowercase letters, however you please. And if you're hearing a hint of Defiance creep back into Dread, you're right, but in some ways Dread is just the fight-or-flight version of our near-constant resistance to mortality.

Here's the thing: dealing with Dread is excruciating. As you grow older you will fall into this "hole which resembles the grave but isn't" time and again. But you can continue to assert your presence and worth just by doing your own "This" every day, however "wild" or small it may seem, even if it's just doing battle with the weeds, like the speaker in Theodore Roethke's "Long Live the Weeds." So your once-lush garden has become an increasingly "narrow vegetable realm," full of "bitter rock" and "barren soil"—so what? So now it's a different kind of garden, but it's still your "realm." You still can create the beautiful, strange "creature" that is you right now, here, in the not-always-dreadful state of growing older:

> Long live the weeds that overwhelm
> My narrow vegetable realm!—
> The bitter rock, the barren soil
> That force the son of man to toil;

*All things unholy, marked by curse,*
*The ugly of the universe,*
*The rough, the wicked, and the wild*
*That keep the spirit undefiled.*
*With these I match my little wit*
*And earn the right to stand or sit,*
*Hope, look, create, or drink and die:*
*These shape the creature that is I.*

# I Don't Have a Pill for That

It scares me to watch
a woman hobble along
the sidewalk, hunched adagio

leaning on—
there's so much fear
I could draw you a diagram

of the great reduction
all of us will soon
be way-back-when.

The wedding is over.
Summer is over.
Life please explain.

This book is nearly halfway read.
I don't have a pill for that,
the doctor said.

—DEBORAH LANDAU

# Bruises

In age, the world grows clumsy.
A heavy jar
leaps from a cupboard.
A suitcase has corners.
Others have no explanation.
Old love, old body,
do you remember—
carpet burns down the spine,
gravel bedding
the knees, hardness to hardness.
You who knew yourself
kissed by the bite of the ant,
you who were kissed by the bite of the spider.
Now kissed by this.

—JANE HIRSHFIELD

# Matins

You want to know how I spend my time?
I walk the front lawn, pretending
to be weeding. You ought to know
I'm never weeding, on my knees, pulling
clumps of clover from the flower beds: in fact
I'm looking for courage, for some evidence
my life will change, though
it takes forever, checking
each clump for the symbolic
leaf, and soon the summer is ending, already
the leaves turning, always the sick trees
going first, the dying turning
brilliant yellow, while a few dark birds perform
their curfew of music. You want to see my hands?
As empty now as at the first note.
Or was the point always
to continue without a sign?

—LOUISE GLÜCK

# Ever

*Never, never, never, never, never.*
—King Lear

Even now I can't grasp "nothing" or "never."
They're unholdable, unglobable, no map to
      nothing.
Never? Never ever again to see you?
An error, I aver. You're never nothing,
because nothing's not a thing.
I know death is absolute, forever,
the guillotine—gutting—never to which we never
      say goodbye.
But even as I think "forever" it goes "ever"
and "ever" and "ever." *Ever after.*
I'm a thing that keeps on thinking. So *I never*
      *see you*

is not a thing or think my mouth can ever. Aver:
You're not "nothing." But neither are you
      something.
Will I ever really *get* never?
You're gone. Nothing, never—ever.

—MEGHAN O'ROURKE

# Lines Written on the Eve of a Birthday

It is the loss of possibility
That claims you bit by bit. They take away
Your man, the children you had hoped would be,
They even take your brown hair and give you gray
Instead. You ask if you can save your face
But that is part of their plan—to strip you
Of your future and put the past in its place.
They don't stop there. They take the skies' deep
      blue
And drain it off; the empty bowl they leave
Inverted, white as bone. They dust the trees
With strontium, but they keep up their sleeve
The biggest trick of all, the one that sees
     You give up in the end. It is the loss
     Of possibility that murders us.

—KELLY CHERRY

# Porcupine Meditation

I used to have tricks, dodges, a whole sackful.
I could outfox anyone,
double back, cover my tracks,
walk backwards, the works.
I left it somewhere, that knack
of running, that good luck.

Now I have only
one trick left: head down, spikes out,
brain tucked in.
I can roll up:
thistle as animal, a flower of quills,
that's about it.

I lie in the grass and watch the sunlight pleating
the skin on the backs of my hands
as if I were a toad, squashed and drying.

I don't even wade through spring water
to cover my scent.
I can't be bothered.

I squat and stink, thinking:
peace and quiet are worth something.
Here I am, dogs,
nose me over,
go away sneezing, snouts full of barbs
hooking their way to your brain.
Now you've got some
of my pain. Much good may it do you.

—MARGARET ATWOOD

# Waking Up

I rise without joy, daub on some rouge,
And force myself to look in the mirror. My face is
    still grey.
I'm gaunt from worry.
I'm desperately lonely. I cry a lot.
At my dressing table, my maid helps blacken my
    eyebrows
And I suffer her to steam my braids.
Plum blossoms for my hair!
She really is an idiot.

—ZHU SHUZHEN (TRANSLATED
BY ADAM LANPHIER)

# Coda

There's little in taking or giving,
There's little in water or wine;
This living, this living, this living
Was never a project of mine.
Oh, hard is the struggle, and sparse is
The gain of the one at the top,
For art is a form of catharsis,
And love is a permanent flop,
And work is the province of cattle,
And rest's for a clam in a shell,
So I'm thinking of throwing the battle—
Would you kindly direct me to hell?

—DOROTHY PARKER

# it was a dream

in which my greater self
rose up before me
accusing me of my life
with her extra finger
whirling in a gyre of rage
at what my days had come to.
what,
i pleaded with her, could i do,
oh what could i have done?
and she twisted her wild hair
and sparked her wild eyes
and screamed as long as
i could hear her
This. This. This.

—LUCILLE CLIFTON

# "Long Live the Weeds"
## *Hopkins*

Long live the weeds that overwhelm
My narrow vegetable realm!—
The bitter rock, the barren soil
That force the son of man to toil;
All things unholy, marked by curse,
The ugly of the universe,
The rough, the wicked, and the wild
That keep the spirit undefiled.
With these I match my little wit
And earn the right to stand or sit,
Hope, look, create, or drink and die:
These shape the creature that is I.

—THEODORE ROETHKE

# Grit

## (WHEN YOU FIND A WAY TO LIVE WITH YOURSELF)

*How did we get so damn old? I say to my
joints, my iron-colored hair. Now I am
older than my love, my departed friends.
Perhaps I will live so long that the New York
Public Library will be obliged to hand over
the walking stick of Virginia Woolf. I would
cherish it for her, and the stones in her pocket.
But I would also keep on living, refusing to
surrender my pen.*

—PATTI SMITH

*At 70 years old, if I could give my younger
self one piece of advice, it would be to use the
words "f\*\*\* off" much more frequently . . .
Growing old is not for pussies—you've got to*

*have courage. But then, you've got to have
courage in life anyway.*

——HELEN MIRREN

*But all the same, there's something about me
that doesn't change, hasn't changed, through
all the remarkable, exciting, alarming, and
disappointing transformations my body has
gone through. There is a person there who
isn't only what she looks like, and to find her
and know her I have to look through, look
in, look deep. Not only in space, but in time.*

URSULA LE GUIN

Ah, that first chin hair, way back when: such
an innocent, impish harbinger of the hell ahead.
You've been through it by now—and the superfi-
cial stuff was the least of it. The worry and stress,
the difficult decisions and wrenching losses, took
you down, yet here you are, frayed and scarred, but
clear-eyed, awake. You're ready, perhaps, to stop
reacting to "aging" and to start living it on your own

terms. As Elizabeth says, exhaling a fragrant cloud of nicotine, "I'm seventy. I can't fuss over chin hairs or gray hairs or frown lines or laugh lines. It's this day, this moment, this *now* that I can own."

Or as Keith Richards said at the Rolling Stones concert where Elizabeth, at age fifty, danced crazily on top of a garbage can, "Happy to be here. Happy to be anywhere." (And Keith *knows*.)

So here's what we hope to give you in this section: poems to help you own this moment—and every one yet to come—like a rock star (a wickedly wizened rock star).

Yeah, claim the stage, seize the day—we know, it sounds good, but trying to put it into practice when you've carried so much anxiety, loss, and social pressure...you're tired before you start. We get it. But you can do this. Like a pushy best friend, the poems in this section invite you to look at yourself afresh, with toughness and compassion, acknowledging what's sad and hard but resolving to move forward with grit and grace. Let the company of these poems help you cultivate a new relationship with aging—not a frenemy battle, not passive complacency, but a hard-won, deeply lived acceptance.

You can start by taking a deep breath and following the suggestion of the Buddhist scripture the *Sutta Nipata*, which is not for the faint of heart:

> *The person who is searching for his own happiness should pull out the dart that he has stuck in himself—the arrow-head of grieving, of desiring, of despair.*

That's right, the dart you stuck in yourself, not the ones "aging while female" has been tossing all these years. It's hard to be a woman growing older in our culture, but you can make the decision to feel better. Stop waiting for the next catastrophe to strike, stop wishing for things you don't really need, and choose to do what brings you authentic joy, no matter how small. Why bemoan your sorry state day after day when, like the woman in "Dawn Revisited," you can "Imagine you wake up / with a second chance" to be who you really want to be:

> *How good to rise in sunlight,*
> *in the prodigal smell of biscuits—*
> *eggs and sausage on the grill.*

Why not wake up and see what's in front of you? Savor the extravagant pleasures of an ordinary day, and see what happens from there.

Sure it takes practice and discipline to notice what's possible, not just what's been lost. But who knows, it might turn out that today "the whole sky is yours // to write on, blown open / to a blank page." As the woman notes:

> ... *You'll never know*
> *who's down there, frying those eggs,*
> *if you don't get up and see.*

See? You're still curious and hungry, eager for good company and hot breakfast. That's the reward of gritting your way toward an acceptance of aging: rediscovering your appetite for life, in all its flaky, yolky lusciousness. And not only that; you'll realize how much you genuinely like yourself, despite—or maybe because of—the changes of "growing older." No longer are you repulsed by your image in the mirror; no longer are you desperate for the approval of others; you're happy now to feast on the life you've created, like the speaker in Derek Walcott's "Love After Love."

This is the fun part, saying amen to the wine and bread of your own heart, coming back into your own, in all your weathered, beat-up glory. Perhaps not every bite of life we take is delicious, and not every moment is grand, but as Edward Field's "People Who Eat in Coffee Shops" reminds us, we're free now to shake off self-consciousness, to indulge ourselves. We can "order the toasted cheese sandwiches blithely, / followed by chocolate egg creams." Why not? As the speaker in Jason Schneiderman's "sugar is smoking" points out, "death / is always around the corner," so why not hide in "the little pleasures / that some of us would go / so far as to say / are the only things / keeping us alive."

But once we come down from the high of our coffee shop glazed donuts, from the giddy liberation of liking our older selves, we crave more sophisticated fare—we want to account thoughtfully for the accomplishments and regrets that have led us, like the woman in Jane Hirshfield's "Mele in Gabbia," to this "good place" in our lives. It's a luxury, but it's work at the same time: resolving to make amends, or make peace, with what you can. Deciding what to hold on to, and what to let go.

That's the joy of being "old enough": you have the perspective now to look back at your life not just with sadness or guilt but also with pride and satisfaction. You have a history now, one you've lived to read unflinchingly and love unconditionally, like the woman in Carolyn Creedon's "Woman, Mined." At the Lord & Taylor makeup counter, the attendant in a "crisp white smock" points out all the damage the woman has done to her skin and says "sternly, *Look what you did.*" But in the photo of her skin, the woman sees not a "mess" but all the late nights and lost loves that have led her right to the place she is now: happy with a man who's like "the best-of-all / flower," happy with the life she's worn her way into. Her face is a jewel, honed and polished by life, she realizes, and she will wear it proudly,

> *with its amber earned, its amethyst, its intaglio tear-*
> *etched diamond, and say,* I am cut that way.

Like shells on the shining Maine beach, we are "all of us, broken, some way," says the woman in Barbara Crooker's "Strewn," but it's a gorgeous

brokenness, "dazzling in the brilliant slanting light."
While those with a "superior aesthetic" might find
us wanting, we unapologetically know and claim
our true selves; like the woman in Barbara Ras' "A
Wife Explains Why She Likes Country," we will
love what we love without shame: boiled peanuts,
big hair, and the gritty truth that "my people / come
from dirt." The same holds true for the woman in
Grace Paley's "Walking in the Woods." Where oth-
ers might simply see a decaying maple tree, she
sees a compatriot, herself, so in love with living she
doesn't mind "the delicious / hospitality of rot," so
long as she can continue to reach toward the sun:

> *the tree not really dying      living*
> *less widely      green head high*
> *above the other leaf-crowded*
> *trees      a terrible stretch to sun*
> *just to stay alive      but if you've*
> *liked life      you do it*

*This* is what we were so afraid of? This is "being
older"? Indulging our sweet tooth, admiring our

proudly broken selves, stretching to the sun? Look, we promise, we're not trying to sugarcoat the reality of life past midlife. It's hard work trying to balance loss and limitation with new freedoms and pleasures. It's tough practicing a healthy, hopeful mind-set. But "if you've / liked life you do it."

We can tell ourselves that "now" is all we have, and we're okay with that; we can claim it's enough to say "my last defense" against age is "the present tense," like the speaker in Gwendolyn Brooks' "Old Mary." And we can try to believe that it doesn't hurt us to know we shall never pursue certain dreams, like "cathedral-hunting in Spain," or "cherrying in Michigan or Maine." But it does hurt. We still want expansive adventures, and many of us will find ways to pursue all of that right up to age one hundred and beyond, no doubt.

But for the rest of us, just doing "What the Living Do," as in Marie Howe's poem, can keep us grounded, if not grateful. "This is the everyday": the clogged sink, the heat on too high, spilling coffee down your arm, noticing the "deep, headstrong blue" of the sky. It's mundane and maddening, but comforting at the same time, these unexpected or hoped-for moments, this "yearning" for more that is our birthright:

> ... *We want the spring to come and the*
> *winter to pass. We want*
> *whoever to call or not call, a letter, a kiss—we*
>     *want more and more and then more of it.*

We want more of the random, ordinary marvels of Frank O'Hara's "Today," things that "really are beautiful!" if we stopped to notice them.

> *Oh! kangaroos, sequins, chocolate sodas!*
> *You really are beautiful! Pearls,*
> *harmonicas, jujubes, aspirins! all*
> *the stuff they've always talked about*
>
> *still makes a poem a surprise!*
> *These things are with us every day*
> *even on beachheads and biers. They*
> *do have meaning. They're strong as rocks.*

Ultimately, these are the things that help us cope with growing older, not the cathedrals in Spain that we'd hoped for, but the magnificent little surprises that make every day a new poem.

That sense of possibility is what carries us from a state of Grit—pushing ourselves toward acceptance—to a state of Grace—loving the world, despite everything. No, we never really expected or wanted to be here: oldish, older, and, dare we say, old. But here we are, and we can choose to hide in an "aging while female" cave, or we can "dwell in Possibility," like rock star Emily Dickinson, in the anything-can-happen poetry of each day. With windows all around us, the roof open to the sky, all we need do each day is spread "wide [our] narrow Hands / To gather Paradise—."

# From the *Sutta Nipata*

The person who is searching for his own happiness should pull out the dart that he has stuck in himself—the arrow-head of grieving, of desiring, of despair.

# Dawn Revisited

Imagine you wake up
with a second chance: The blue jay
hawks his pretty wares
and the oak still stands, spreading
glorious shade. If you don't look back,

the future never happens.
How good to rise in sunlight,
in the prodigal smell of biscuits—
eggs and sausage on the grill.
The whole sky is yours

to write on, blown open
to a blank page. Come on,
shake a leg! You'll never know
who's down there, frying those eggs,
if you don't get up and see.

—RITA DOVE

# Love After Love

The time will come
when, with elation,
you will greet yourself arriving
at your own door, in your own mirror,
and each will smile at the other's welcome,

and say, sit here. Eat.
You will love again the stranger who was your self.
Give wine. Give bread. Give back your heart
to itself, to the stranger who has loved you

all your life, whom you ignored
for another, who knows you by heart.
Take down the love letters from the bookshelf,

the photographs, the desperate notes,
peel your own image from the mirror.
Sit. Feast on your life.

—DEREK WALCOTT

# People Who Eat in Coffee Shops

People who eat in coffee shops
are not worried about nutrition.
They order the toasted cheese sandwiches blithely,
followed by chocolate egg creams and plaster of
        paris
wedges of lemon meringue pie.
They don't have parental, dental, or medical
        figures hovering
full of warnings, or whip out dental floss
        immediately.
They can live in furnished rooms and whenever
        they want
go out and eat glazed donuts along with
        innumerable coffees,
dousing their cigarettes in sloppy saucers.

—EDWARD FIELD

# sugar is smoking

it's amazing how death
is always around the corner,
or not even so far away
as that, hiding in the little pleasures
that some of us would go
so far as to say
are the only things
keeping us alive

—JASON SCHNEIDERMAN

# Caroline County

One green grove
backlit by
late light.
Could I be
docile, soft
like biscuit dough?
(Knead me.)
Would I wipe
the glimmer
of grease
off the kitchen
walls?
Or wait?
Wishing, smoking.

—ELIZABETH ASH VÉLEZ

# Mele in Gabbia

The pastry
is dusted with sugar.
The slices of apple inside,
just sour enough.

The name,
"apples in a cage."

I eat them
in this good place—
the pastry warm,
a little bit chewy,
the linen
impeccably white—
and consider.

—JANE HIRSHFIELD

# Woman, Mined

In the cosmetics department of Lord & Taylor
they'll take you right there, right out in the open,
plain as day, and snap you with an ultraviolet
      camera,
show you what you've done to your skin just
by living, your face exposed suddenly like what's
really going on under a lifted-up log, the real you
you are, caught and pinned like a moth,
like a shoplifter, like a woman on a table

and the lady in the crisp white smock will expertly
flick the snapshot in front of you, laid out
like a color-coded map of conquered countries,
the purples and browns places you gave up
without a care in your twenties, to late nights
and poolside deck chairs and men, all the men
you touched, the ones who marked you, whose
      traces

you bear, and now you can see the archaeology
of tears, their white-acid trails, and the lady
will say, sternly, *Look what you did*

and you will see the mess of it you made, and you
will see the times when you carelessly went to bed
with someone without the proper moisturizer,
       when you
suckled that man like a baby, and when you moved
with another like a girl on a rocker until you fell off
and lost him, and finally picked another, like the
       best-of-all
flower, and kept him, cried on him, made him
       sandwiches,
made him a baby, and you'll wear your face
with its amber earned, its amethyst, its intaglio
       tear-
etched diamond, and say, *I am cut that way.*

—CAROLYN CREEDON

# Strewn

It'd been a long winter, rags of snow hanging on;
     then, at the end
of April, an icy nor'easter, powerful as a hurricane.
     But now
I've landed on the coast of Maine, visiting a friend
     who lives
two blocks from the ocean, and I can't believe my
     luck,
out this mild morning, race-walking along the
     strand.
Every dog within fifty miles is off-leash, running
for the sheer dopey joy of it. No one's in the water,
but walkers and shellers leave their tracks on the
     hardpack.
The flat sand shines as if varnished in a painting.
     Underfoot,
strewn, are broken bits and pieces, deep indigo
     mussels, whorls

of whelk, chips of purple and white wampum,
       hinges of quahog,
fragments of sand dollars. Nothing whole,
       everything
broken, washed up here, stranded. The light
       pours down, a rinse
of lemon on a cold plate. All of us, broken,
       some way
or other. All of us dazzling in the brilliant slanting
       light.

—BARBARA CROOKER

# A Wife Explains Why
# She Likes Country

Because those cows in the bottomland are black
      and white, colors
anyone can understand, even against the green
of the grass, where they glide like yes and no,
      nothing in between,
because in country, heartache has nowhere to hide,
it's the Church of Abundant Life, the Alamo,
the hubbub of the hoi polloi, the parallel lines of
      rail fences,
because I like rodeos more than golf,
because there's something about the sound of
      mealworms and
leeches and the dream of a double-wide
that reminds me this is America, because of the
      simple pleasure
of a last chance, because sometimes whiskey
tastes better than wine, because hauling hogs on
      the road

is as good as it gets when the big bodies are layered
        like pigs in a cake,
not one layer but two,
because only country has a gun with a full choke
        and a slide guitar
that melts playing it cool into sweaty surrender in
        one note,
because in country you can smoke forever and it'll
        never kill you,
because roadbeds, flatbeds, your bed or mine,
because the package store is right across from the
        chicken plant
and it sells boiled peanuts, because I'm fixin' to
        wear boots to the dance
and make my hair bigger, because no smarty-pants,
        just easy rhymes,
perfect love, because I'm lost deep within myself
        and the sad songs call me out,
because even you with your superior aesthetic cried
when Tammy Wynette died,
because my people
come from dirt.

—BARBARA RAS

# Walking in the Woods

That's when I saw the old maple
a couple of its thick arms cracked
one arm reclining half rotted
into earth      black with the delicious
hospitality of rot to the
littlest creatures

the tree not really dying      living
less widely      green head high
above the other leaf-crowded
trees   a terrible stretch to sun
just to stay alive      but if you've
liked life      you do it

—GRACE PALEY

# Old Mary

My last defense
Is the present tense

It little hurts me now to know
I shall not go

Cathedral-hunting in Spain
Nor cherrying in Michigan or Maine

—GWENDOLYN BROOKS

# What the Living Do

Johnny, the kitchen sink has been clogged for days,
      some utensil probably fell down there.
And the Drano won't work but smells dangerous,
      and the crusty dishes have piled up

waiting for the plumber I still haven't called.
      This is the everyday we spoke of.
It's winter again: the sky's a deep, headstrong
      blue, and the sunlight pours through

the open living-room windows because the heat's
      on too high in here and I can't turn it off.
For weeks now, driving, or dropping a bag of
      groceries in the street, the bag breaking,

I've been thinking: This is what the living do. And
      yesterday, hurrying along those
wobbly bricks in the Cambridge sidewalk, spilling
      my coffee down my wrist and sleeve,

I thought it again, and again later, when buying a
      hairbrush: This is it.
Parking. Slamming the car door shut in the cold.
      What you called that yearning.

What you finally gave up. We want the spring to
      come and the winter to pass. We want
whoever to call or not call, a letter, a kiss—we want
      more and more and then more of it.

But there are moments, walking, when I catch a
      glimpse of myself in the window glass,
say, the window of the corner video store, and I'm
      gripped by a cherishing so deep

for my own blowing hair, chapped face, and
      unbuttoned coat that I'm speechless:
I am living. I remember you.

—MARIE HOWE

# Today

Oh! kangaroos, sequins, chocolate sodas!
You really are beautiful! Pearls,
harmonicas, jujubes, aspirins! all
the stuff they've always talked about

still makes a poem a surprise!
These things are with us every day
even on beachheads and biers. They
do have meaning. They're strong as rocks.

—FRANK O'HARA

# I dwell in Possibility

I dwell in Possibility—
A fairer House than Prose—
More numerous of Windows—
Superior—for Doors—

Of Chambers as the Cedars—
Impregnable of eye—
And for an Everlasting Roof
The Gambrels of the Sky—

Of Visitors—the fairest—
For Occupation—This—
The spreading wide my narrow Hands
To gather Paradise—

—EMILY DICKINSON

# Grace

## (WHEN YOU FIND A WAY TO LIVE IN THE WORLD)

*Caring for myself is not self-indulgence, it
is self-preservation, and that is an act of
political warfare.*

—AUDRE LORDE

*And there's an ideal beauty that is harder to
define or understand, because it occurs not
just in the body but where the body
and the spirit meet and define each
other . . . I see, for a moment, all that at
once, I glimpse what no mirror can reflect,
the spirit flashing out across the years,
beautiful. That must be what the great
artists see and paint. That must be
why the tired, aged faces in Rembrandt's*

> *portraits give us such delight: they show us beauty not skin-deep but life-deep.*

> —URSULA LE GUIN

We promised we'd get you through Insult (that's not my face in the mirror), through Injury (bodily malfunctions), and through the Dread (dusty death) that follows us as we age and change. We've pumped you up in Defiance (Madonna's glorious battle cry, "f*ck you, I'm 50"), and pushed you forward in Grit ("if you've / liked life you do it"). We know you may not go through these stages all at once or in any one order. But we hope you'll visit this last one sooner rather than later, and often: the stage of Grace, where you feel truly at peace in what poet Ada Limón calls "the conditional"—"us alive, / right here, feeling lucky."

Elizabeth can finally come to terms with the notion that seventy is indeed terminal—miniskirts have been tossed, and the mirror is rapidly losing its power. And Mary, whose hallmark (says Elizabeth, while Mary rolls her eyes) has always been radiant goldenness—hair, skin, eyes, soul—may

finally accept that her spirit will "flash out" beauti-
fully, forever, despite her *Harriet the Spy* duds.

In the glorious light of Grace we see with relief
that "the loss of possibility" has not quite mur-
dered us. In fact, as Dickinson joyfully reminds us,
we dwell in the fair house of possibility, roof open
to the sky and light. In her tornado-shaped poem,
"Coming Up Into the Light," Julie Williams states,
"You can only hunker down so long & then the
wind dies." The storm passes, and you're left

> *hoping with a deep longing*
> *the wind has cleared*
> *the air &*
>
> *the new*
> *light*
> *shining*
> *is*
> *there*
> *to*
> *stay*

It's not that everything is easy now that we are
finally "old." The storm will not necessarily set

us down in the Land of Oz with our ruby slippers and three best friends (that was *Sex and the City*). Our bodies may drag, may hurt, and certainly are creased and mapped by the lives we've led. But as Anne Lamott says, "Your inside person is soul, is heart, in the eternal now, the ageless, the old, the young, all the ages you've ever been."

We come up into the light through our own darkness, like the woman in Marie Howe's "The Gate." Though devastated by our losses we somehow learn to live in the space they've left behind, as if by going on we can keep alive their spirit and sensibilities. As the woman says: "I had no idea that the gate I would step through / to finally enter this world // would be the space my brother's body made." Her lost brother, "done at twenty-eight, having folded every sheet, // rinsed every glass he would ever rinse," has made it necessary for her to live fully in the world, carrying with her the gift of his joy and spirit:

> *This is what you have been waiting for, he used to*
> *say to me.*
> *And I'd say, What?*

*And he'd say, This—holding up my cheese and*
    *mustard sandwich.*
*And I'd say, What?*

*And he'd say, This, sort of looking around.*

Like the "greater self" from Lucille Clifton's "it was a dream," the lost brother calls his sister to see what's in front of her, this extraordinary ordinary bread of life, this here-and-now world.

That's what we're called to do, too: stop looking for choirs of angels dropping out of the sky and enter instead into the "cheese and mustard" grace of the everyday. When we practice the art of "sort of looking around," we just may find glorious peace in unexpected places, like the speaker in James Wright's "Milkweed." Lost in regret or grief, the man stands looking at a view he's too distracted to really see. Then his hand brushes against a milkweed pod, releasing its silky white down into the air, and suddenly:

*. . . It is all changed.*
*Whatever it was I lost, whatever I wept for*

*Was a wild, gentle thing, the small dark eyes*
*Loving me in secret.*
*It is here. At a touch of my hand,*
*The air fills with delicate creatures*
*From the other world.*

The past he was stuck in becomes the magnificent present, a visitation of wafting, earthly angels. He realizes the "wild, gentle thing" he lost is "here" with him, and has been all along, "loving [him] in secret."

Just by noticing and reaching out to the world, even in an accidental "sort of" way, we brush up against a grace that can sustain, even transform, these days of growing older. We have lost much, but we can still have much—if we "make the time" to really see the battering beauty of the world, as in Seamus Heaney's "Postscript." The speaker visits County Clare, Ireland, in autumnal "September or October," like this stage of life, a blustery season

*... when the wind*
*And the light are working off each other*
*So that the ocean on one side is wild*

*With foam and glitter, and inland among stones*
*The surface of a slate-grey lake is lit*
*By the earthed lightning of a flock of swans*

In the swans, the speaker sees himself, sees us all in the "earthed lightning" of our later years: our "feathers roughed and ruffling," lashed by the "foam and glitter" of the wild ocean, our "fully grown headstrong-looking heads / Tucked or cresting or busy underwater." This is what he came to see, what we all might see if we lift our faces to the world and allow grace to "catch the heart off guard and blow it open." In that moment, the speaker is "neither here nor there," but he is connected, somehow, to everything. That's what we hope you can find and feel, despite all the limitations and losses of a long life—the "big soft buffetings" of grace that come at you "sideways" and reveal the splendor of the world you still very much inhabit.

And this feeling doesn't have to rely on such specific conditions as heading to County Clare, Ireland in autumn and hoping you'll catch that light and wind and those swans—it means being open in every moment, like the woman in Ada Limón's

"The Conditional." So what if tomorrow doesn't come or the solar system erupts in a "foul black tire fire," and we wind up spending our last moments "staring / at each other, hands knotted together, / clutching the dog, watching the sky burn." Somehow, mysteriously, we could still find joy, says the woman:

> *Say, It doesn't matter. Say, That would be*
> *enough. Say you'd still want this: us alive,*
> *right here, feeling lucky.*

Can it be true? Can we really be suckered into thinking that the world could be ending and we'd be happy just to be with those we loved, just to have lived with one another and our ever-loyal dogs in this lucky world? Yes, we say yes, in our best Molly Bloom, we say yes, it is possible, yes, as in Ruth Stone's "Green Apples":

> *The green apples fell on the sloping roof*
> *And rattled down.*
> *The wind was shaking me all night long;*
> *Shaking me in my sleep*

*Like a definition of love,*
*Saying, this is the moment,*
*Here, now.*

We've waged personal, interior struggles with aging, from the shock of our changing faces and bodies, to regrets and tragedies that have shattered and numbed our hearts, but somehow—who knows how, exactly—we find strength to head outward into the world, to work and laugh and challenge ourselves still, to risk love and adventure (from the comfort of our orthopedic shoes). We can cherish a rattling, shaking joy of loving and being loved, of having done some part of our lives well, like the father in Thomas Lux's "A Little Tooth," whose baby daughter grows into a woman in three short stanzas:

*. . . You did, you loved, your feet*
*are sore. It's dusk. Your daughter's tall.*

What a relief in Grace, to be "old, flyblown" and still to "rue / nothing," to not tally the painful losses but instead to bask in what you've done well. We can cling to fear and worry, or we can feel proud of our best moments, and move forward hopefully, cultivating a perspective of wonder and acceptance, like Prospero in Shakespeare's *The Tempest*. His daughter, too, has just grown toward liberated adulthood (despite his flawed parenting), and now with bittersweet clarity he sees the world as beautiful in its brevity:

> *... The cloud-capp'd towers, the gorgeous palaces,*
> *The solemn temples, the great globe itself,*
> *Yea, all which it inherit, shall dissolve*
> *And, like this insubstantial pageant faded,*
> *Leave not a rack behind. We are such stuff*
> *As dreams are made on, and our little life*
> *Is rounded with a sleep.*

A dreamy sleep after a "cloud-capp'd" little life— not such a bad way to view death, and not a bad way to practice facing it. Perhaps what cynical poet Philip Larkin said is true: "What will survive of us is love." Perhaps Walt Whitman has it right in *Song of Myself*:

*All goes onward and outward, nothing collapses,*
*And to die is different from what any one supposed,*
*    and luckier.*

Maybe we really can go out, not in an action-movie blaze of glory, but in a "final flood of colors" from our still brightly shining world. Perhaps in this stage of living—and dying—we can find comfort in the "gorgeous palaces" of the everyday, as in Clive James' "Japanese Maple" (written during his struggle with cancer). Slowly "fading out" from illness, the man sees from his bed the newly planted Japanese maple tree and thinks:

*... When did you ever see*
*So much sweet beauty as when fine rain falls*
*On that small tree*
*And saturates your brick back garden walls,*
*So many Amber Rooms and mirror halls?*

His world isn't diminished; it's expanded, enhanced, and his garden appears as a palace "ever more lavish as the dusk descends." "This glistening

illuminates the air," he observes. "It never ends."
From his sickbed he will live to see the maple tree
in autumn, when "its leaves will turn to flame,"
and he's comforted knowing that until then—and
forever after—the brilliant world "continues all the
same":

> *Filling the double doors to bathe my eyes,*
> *A final flood of colors will live on*
> *As my mind dies,*
> *Burned by my vision of a world that shone*
> *So brightly at the last, and then was gone.*

Whether or not we believe in something tran-
scendent or spiritual, and even when we're faced
with sickness and worse, we still can acknowledge
the blazing beauty of the world, and find ourselves
in a state of awe. In Wallace Stevens' "Of Mere
Being," the speaker considers what life comes down
to in the end, at "the end of the mind, / Beyond the
last thought." Is there some revelation of love, as in
"Milkweed," or is there only a "gold-feathered bird"
that sings "without human meaning, / Without

human feeling, a foreign song"? Stevens suggests it's up to us to find meaning in the "mere being" of our lives, but he leaves us with a triumphant image of (what we see as) spiritual majesty:

*The palm stands on the edge of space.*
*The wind moves slowly in the branches.*
*The bird's fire-fangled feathers dangle down.*

As "mere beings" we are human, not "just" women, yes, but guess what? Ha! Oh! Kangaroos and sequins, it turns out our experience of "aging while female" just may have given us an edge in the "what's it all about" angst of older age. All of those insults and injuries, all the dread, defiance, grit, helped us cultivate the grace that steadies us now. We know it's not just about the fire-fangled feathers at the end of life; it's about the fire-fangled *life*, the glistening, illuminated world we create throughout our lives as women—body, heart, and soul. We learned early—we had to learn—that when the body and the spirit come together, as Ursula Le Guin says, we get to beauty that is "not skin-deep but life-deep":

*My mother died at eighty-three, of cancer, in pain, her spleen enlarged so that her body was misshapen. Is that the person I see when I think of her? Sometimes. I wish it were not. It is a true image, yet it blurs, it clouds, a truer image. It is one memory among fifty years of memories of my mother... Beneath it, behind it is a deeper, complex, ever-changing image, made from imagination, hearsay, photographs, memories. I see a little red-haired child in the mountains of Colorado, a sad-faced, delicate college girl, a kind, smiling young mother, a brilliantly intellectual woman, a peerless flirt, a serious artist, a splendid cook—I see her rocking, weeding, writing, laughing—I see the turquoise bracelets on her delicate, freckled arm—I see, for a moment, all that at once, I glimpse what no mirror can reflect, the spirit flashing out across the years, beautiful.*

This is what the mother in Margaret Atwood's "Solstice Poem, iv" wants for her daughter, a life-deep truth she translates into this advice for living (which is neither fairy tale nor horror movie, not an ideal of a brightly shining world but a real one):

*I would like to tell her, Love*
*is enough, I would like to say,*
*Find shelter in another skin.*

*I would like to say, Dance*
*and be happy. Instead I will say*
*in my crone's voice, Be*
*ruthless when you have to, tell*
*the truth when you can,*
*when you can see it.*

*Iron talismans, and ugly, but*
*more loyal than mirrors.*

We see Atwood's poem—and all the poems in this book—as talismans against the bias and self-doubt, the sorrow and fear of growing older as women. Read them out loud, memorize them—yeah, okay, tweet, pin, and text them, too. Talk about aging that's scary and weird and joyful bit by bit and all at once.

The hell with shame and silence—we've come through aging together, and we can continue to share it through poems like Grace Paley's "Here."

The woman in the garden asks "how did this happen," this life that's left us gnawed and nibbled and patched up and ebullient and grateful, this life that's left us "an old woman with heavy breasts / and a nicely mapped face." Her answer is what we can carry with us every day: "well that's who I wanted to be."

# Coming Up Into the Light

You can only hunker down so long & then the wind dies
or rushes on to some other place to do its damage
& all that time you've been huddled there together
holding your breath, hoping against

wildest hope that up aboveground
nothing you love has been
blown away

hoping with a deep longing
the wind has cleared
the air &

the new
light
shining
is
there
to
stay

—JULIE WILLIAMS

# The Gate

I had no idea that the gate I would step through
to finally enter this world

would be the space my brother's body made. He was
a little taller than me: a young man

but grown, himself by then,
done at twenty-eight, having folded every sheet,

rinsed every glass he would ever rinse under the
      cold
and running water.

This is what you have been waiting for, he used
      to say to me.
And I'd say, What?

And he'd say, This—holding up my cheese and
      mustard sandwich.
And I'd say, What?

And he'd say, This, sort of looking around.

—MARIE HOWE

# Milkweed

While I stood here, in the open, lost in myself,
I must have looked a long time
Down the corn rows, beyond grass,
The small house,
White walls, animals lumbering toward the barn.
I look down now. It is all changed.
Whatever it was I lost, whatever I wept for
Was a wild, gentle thing, the small dark eyes
Loving me in secret.
It is here. At a touch of my hand,
The air fills with delicate creatures
From the other world.

—JAMES WRIGHT

# Postscript

And some time make the time to drive out west
Into County Clare, along the Flaggy Shore,
In September or October, when the wind
And the light are working off each other
So that the ocean on one side is wild
With foam and glitter, and inland among stones
The surface of a slate-grey lake is lit
By the earthed lightning of a flock of swans,
Their feathers roughed and ruffling, white on white,
Their fully grown headstrong-looking heads
Tucked or cresting or busy underwater.
Useless to think you'll park and capture it
More thoroughly. You are neither here nor there,
A hurry through which known and strange things
        pass
As big soft buffetings come at the car sideways
And catch the heart off guard and blow it open.

—SEAMUS HEANEY

# The Conditional

Say tomorrow doesn't come.
Say the moon becomes an icy pit.
Say the sweet-gum tree is petrified.
Say the sun's a foul black tire fire.
Say the owl's eyes are pinpricks.
Say the raccoon's a hot tar stain.
Say the shirt's plastic ditch-litter.
Say the kitchen's a cow's corpse.
Say we never get to see it: bright
future, stuck like a bum star, never
coming close, never dazzling.
Say we never meet her. Never him.
Say we spend our last moments staring
at each other, hands knotted together,
clutching the dog, watching the sky burn.
Say, It doesn't matter. Say, That would be
enough. Say you'd still want this: us alive,
right here, feeling lucky.

—ADA LIMÓN

# Green Apples

In August we carried the old horsehair mattress
To the back porch
And slept with our children in a row.
The wind came up the mountain into the orchard
Telling me something:
Saying something urgent.
I was happy.
The green apples fell on the sloping roof
And rattled down.
The wind was shaking me all night long;
Shaking me in my sleep
Like a definition of love,
Saying, this is the moment,
Here, now.

—RUTH STONE

# A Little Tooth

Your baby grows a tooth, then two,
and four, and five, then she wants some meat
directly from the bone. It's all

over: she'll learn some words, she'll fall
in love with cretins, dolts, a sweet
talker on his way to jail. And you,

your wife, get old, flyblown, and rue
nothing. You did, you loved, your feet
are sore. It's dusk. Your daughter's tall.

—THOMAS LUX

# From *The Tempest*

Our revels now are ended. These our actors,
As I foretold you, were all spirits and
Are melted into air, into thin air:
And, like the baseless fabric of this vision,
The cloud-capp'd towers, the gorgeous palaces,
The solemn temples, the great globe itself,
Yea, all which it inherit, shall dissolve
And, like this insubstantial pageant faded,
Leave not a rack behind. We are such stuff
As dreams are made on, and our little life
Is rounded with a sleep.

—WILLIAM SHAKESPEARE

# From *Song of Myself*

I wish I could translate the hints about the dead
      young men and women,
And the hints about old men and mothers, and the
      offspring taken soon out of their laps.

What do you think has become of the young and
      old men?
And what do you think has become of the women
      and children?

They are alive and well somewhere,
The smallest sprout shows there is really no death,
And if ever there was it led forward life,
      and does not wait at the end to arrest it,
And ceas'd the moment life appear'd.

All goes onward and outward, nothing collapses,
And to die is different from what any one
      supposed, and luckier.

—WALT WHITMAN

# Japanese Maple

Your death, near now, is of an easy sort.
So slow a fading out brings no real pain.
Breath growing short
Is just uncomfortable. You feel the drain
Of energy, but thought and sight remain:

Enhanced, in fact. When did you ever see
So much sweet beauty as when fine rain falls
On that small tree
And saturates your brick back garden walls,
So many Amber Rooms and mirror halls?

Ever more lavish as the dusk descends
This glistening illuminates the air.
It never ends.
Whenever the rain comes it will be there,
Beyond my time, but now I take my share.

My daughter's choice, the maple tree is new.
Come autumn and its leaves will turn to flame.
What I must do
Is live to see that. That will end the game
For me, though life continues all the same:

Filling the double doors to bathe my eyes,
A final flood of colors will live on
As my mind dies,
Burned by my vision of a world that shone
So brightly at the last, and then was gone.

—CLIVE JAMES

# Of Mere Being

The palm at the end of the mind,
Beyond the last thought, rises
In the bronze decor,

A gold-feathered bird
Sings in the palm, without human meaning,
Without human feeling, a foreign song.

You know then that it is not the reason
That makes us happy or unhappy.
The bird sings. Its feathers shine.

The palm stands on the edge of space.
The wind moves slowly in the branches.
The bird's fire-fangled feathers dangle down.

—WALLACE STEVENS

# Solstice Poem, iv

My daughter crackles paper, blows
on the tree to make it live, festoons
herself with silver.
So far she has no use
for gifts.

What can I give her,
what armor, invincible
sword or magic trick, when that year comes?

How can I teach her
some way of being human
that won't destroy her?

I would like to tell her, Love
is enough, I would like to say,
Find shelter in another skin.

I would like to say, Dance
and be happy. Instead I will say
in my crone's voice, Be
ruthless when you have to, tell
the truth when you can,
when you can see it.

Iron talismans, and ugly, but
more loyal than mirrors.

—MARGARET ATWOOD

# Here

Here I am in the garden laughing
an old woman with heavy breasts
and a nicely mapped face

how did this happen
well that's who I wanted to be

at last    a woman
in the old style    sitting
stout thighs apart under
a big skirt    grandchild sliding
on    off my lap    a pleasant
summer perspiration

that's my old man across the yard
he's talking to the meter reader
he's telling him the world's sad story
how electricity is oil or uranium
and so forth    I tell my grandson

run over to your grandpa    ask him
to sit beside me for a minute    I
am suddenly exhausted by my desire
to kiss his sweet explaining lips.

—GRACE PALEY

# Authors' Note and Afterword

*Found poems take existing texts and refashion them, reorder them, and present them as poems.*

(THE AMERICAN ACADEMY OF POETS)

*Happy poets who write found poetry go pawing through popular culture like sculptors on trash heaps. They hold and wave aloft usable artifacts and fragments: jingles and ad copy, menus and broadcasts—all objets trouvés, the literary equivalents of Warhol's Campbell's soup cans and Duchamp's bicycle. By entering a found text as a poem, the poet doubles its*

> *context. The original meaning remains*
> *intact, but now it swings between two poles.*
> *The poet adds, or at any rate increases, the*
> *element of delight.*

(ANNIE DILLARD, *MORNINGS LIKE THIS:*
*FOUND POEMS*)

Our goal in *How Did This Happen?* was to find poetry that speaks to women's lived experience of growing older. We found that not just in strictly defined poetry, from Emily Dickinson to Rita Dove, but also in the tweets, sketches, memoirs, interviews, and fiction of strong, eloquent women like Sarah Silverman, Frances McDormand, and Jenny Offill.

In their words we heard echoes of Dorothy Parker, Louise Glück, Margaret Atwood, and Ada Limón, among others. So we included fragments of their work, word for word, sometimes as quotations and epigraphs, and sometimes as "found poems" with titles, line breaks, and spacing that highlight their poetic power—like "42 AND Female" (from a Sarah Silverman tweet) and "Laugh Lines" (from an interview with Frances McDormand).

We wanted to show that *this* is how women voice their experience of aging in our modern culture, right now—with in-your-face honesty, sharp humor, resonant social critique, and deeply moving beauty. We sought to distill and condense that into the poetry that their work really is, setting their voices in dialogue with legendary poets like Lucille Clifton and Marie Howe, Claudia Emerson and Gwendolyn Brooks. We envisioned all of them together having one down-and-dirty, brilliant, rollicking, sobering, comforting conversation about growing older. A living collection of women poets trading ideas and ribbing one another and telling the truth, in an intimate but shared way, about what it means to age as a woman.

We could (and do) say to friends who are coping with growing older, "Check out this magazine article here, and this YouTube clip over there, and read pages *x* and *y* of this book." But it's like throwing a dinner party, or holding a meeting of activists—you want to call everyone together in the same place and let them get to know one another, share their stories, get fired up and calmed down, find common purpose and comfort and inspiration. That's what's behind our epigraphs, quotations, and "found poetry."

It's like our poetry version of Judy Chicago's *The Dinner Party*, in a way, not that we're saying we're on Judy Chicago's level. But we are paying homage to those who have articulated for us what we find so hard to express ourselves: that aging as a woman in this culture can feel both disruptive and revelatory, absurdly oppressive and surprisingly liberating.

Through this gathering of women, we hope our readers will begin to see poetry—classic and found—all around them. Because we truly believe in the power of poetry to transform our lives, to help us get through the heartbreak of being alive.

# Permissions

We are immensely grateful to the rights holders who have worked so closely with us to clear permissions for our anthology. Poets, publishing houses, agents, and estates have responded to our requests with generosity and support. We particularly would like to thank Fred Courtright, of The Permissions Company, Inc., who has stayed with us throughout this long and complicated process. We have worked carefully to include all grantors; if we have overlooked anyone, please accept our heartfelt apology. We will include any omissions in future editions.

# Citations

**INTRODUCTION**

Ephron, Nora. *I Feel Bad About My Neck: And Other Thoughts on Being a Woman*. New York, NY: Vintage, 2008. Print.

Laing, Olivia. *The Lonely City: Adventures in the Art of Being Alone*. New York, NY: Picador, 2016. Print.

Weiner, Jennifer. "The Pressure to Look Good." *New York Times,* May 30, 2015: Sunday Review. Print.

Burns, Caroline. "A Chat with Poet Jane Hirshfield." *The Washington Post*, May 13, 2015: Books. Online.

## INSULT

Leonard, Elizabeth. "Amy Poehler on Life and Looks: 'I Don't Like Pretending Things Are Perfect.'" *People*, October 22, 2014. Online.

Silverman, Sarah (sarahksilverman). "Oh my gosh I'm embarrassed. i just found out I'm a woman AND I'm 42. I am so sorry." 6 Sep. 2013, 12:12 AM Tweet.

Morrison, Toni. *The Bluest Eye*. New York, NY: Vintage, 2007. Print.

Fey, Tina. *Bossypants*. New York, NY: Regan Arthur Books/Little, Brown and Company, Hachette Book Group, 2011. Print.

Bee, Samantha. "Why Samantha Bee Wants to Age Ungracefully." *Chatelaine*, April 2013. Online.

## INJURY

Moran, Caitlin. *How to Be a Woman*. New York, NY: Harper Perennial, 2012. Print.

Ephron, Nora. *I Feel Bad About My Neck: And Other Thoughts on Being a Woman*. New York, NY: Vintage, 2008. Print.

Offill, Jenny. *Dept. of Speculation*. New York, NY: Vintage Contemporaries, 2014. Print.

Sawer, Patrick. "Judi Dench: 'There's Nothing Good About Being 80—Bugger the Wealth of Knowledge.'" *The Telegraph*. Telegraph Media Group Limited, 7 March 2015. Online.

Shire, Warsan. "what they did yesterday afternoon." *Teaching My Mother How to Give Birth*. London: flipped eye publishing limited; Mouthmark edition, 2011.

Fisher, M.F.K. *Sister Age*. New York, NY: Vintage; 9 edition, 1984. Print.

## DEFIANCE

Bruni, Frank. "A Star Who Has No Time for Vanity." *New York Times*, October 15, 2014. Online.

Gay, Jason. "Beyoncé Knowles: The Queen B." *Vogue,* February 11, 2013. Online.

Madonna. "Up Close and Personal with Madonna." Interview by Cynthia McFadden. ABC News *Nightline*. May 22, 2008.

Lennon, Christine. "Forever 21: The Antiaging Secrets of Jennifer Lopez and 40-Something Actresses." *W.* 12 January 2016. Online.

McDormand, Frances. "Frances McDormand Talks About Her Role as Olive Kitteridge." Interview by Katie Couric. Yahoo! News. October 29, 2014.

Smith, Zadie. "A Conversation with Zadie Smith." Penguin Books USA Readers' Guide to Zadie Smith's *On Beauty*. Penguin Group USA, 2016. Online.

## DREAD

Yeats, William Butler. From "The Tower," part I, lines 1–4.

Rich, Adrienne. From "Contradictions: Tracking Poems," Poem #18, "The problem, unstated till now, is how." *Your Native Land, Your Life*. New York, NY: W.W. Norton & Company, Inc., 1986.

Shakespeare, William. *Macbeth*. From "Tomorrow, and tomorrow, and tomorrow" soliloquy, V, v, 23–24.

Larkin, Philip. From "Aubade." *Collected Poems*. Farrar, Straus and Giroux, LLC., 2001.

# GRIT

Smith, Patti. *M Train*. New York, NY: Penguin Random House, 2016.

Mirren, Helen. "'I Don't Give a Damn about Getting Older...I Get Snapped on the Bus with No Make-up on': Helen Mirren on Age and Sexuality." Interview by Bella Blissett for *You* magazine. *UK Daily Mail Online*, September 12, 2015.

Le Guin, Ursula. *The Wave in the Mind*. Boulder, CO: Shambhala Publications, 2004. Print.

# GRACE

Lorde, Audre. *A Burst of Light: Essays*. Ithaca, NY: Firebrand Books, First Edition, 1988.

Le Guin, Ursula. *The Wave in the Mind*. Boulder, CO: Shambhala Publications, 2004. Print.

Hepola, Sarah. "Anne Lamott: 'We Stuffed Scary Feelings Down, and They Made Us Insane.'" *Salon*, November 3, 2014. Online.

Larkin, Philip. From "An Arundel Tomb." *Collected Poems*. Farrar, Straus and Giroux, LLC., 2001.

## AUTHORS' NOTE AND AFTERWORD

"Found Poem: Poetic Form" from Poets.org. Academy of American Poets, August 25, 2016. Online.

Dillard, Annie. *Mornings Like This: Found Poems*. New York, NY: Harper Perennial Reprint edition, 1996. Print.

# Acknowledgments

Special thanks to our amazing agent, Miriam Altshuler, ♥ and to Reiko Davis, for their perseverance and support. Thanks also to our indefatigable editor, Millicent Bennett, and the team at Grand Central, including Jessica Pierce (preternaturally patient); Shelby Howick, Brian McLendon; our eagle-eyed copy editor, Eileen Chetti (Eileen! Holy smokes, you saved us); and our heaven-sent production editor, Siri Silleck. Thanks more than we can say to all the permissions grantors who worked so hard on our behalf. We are indebted to Dawn Porter, Lizz Winstead, Sarah Silverman, Frances McDormand, Deborah Landau, Fred Courtright, Jane Friedman, Molly Chehak, Kak Slick, Charlene Brown-McKenzie, Dennis Williams, Pam Fox, Barbara Cohn, Renee Blalock, Devita Bishundat, Mike Hochberger, Shelley Dropkin, Kate Bennis, Jim Esselman and Diana Merelman,

Julie Convisser, Alison Kuhn, Bonnie Duncan, Ian Dillard, Marion Wheeler, Brazos Tacos, Juice Laundry, C-ville friends and neighbors, MC Belford (aka Megan Clifford, photographer extraordinaire), and Sue Clifford (in fact, *all* of those Cliffords).

Mary thanks her parents for everything and her brilliant sister, Julie Esselman Tomz, for critiquing (and connecting) across time zones and busy lives. Thank you, Rachel Lalljee Gyves (I'm waving!).

This book would not have been possible without Mary's husband, Greg, who provided the subtitle, Mary's author photo, first reads of every draft, and more love, fun, creativity, tenderness, and forbearance than Mary can describe, let alone live up to. Mary is also beholden to her son, Luke, a true poet, a bright light, a beautiful soul: "i carry your heart (i carry it in my heart)."

Elizabeth thanks Larry as always—just fifty-three years since that "very dry" martini and Staten Island Ferry ride (how did *that* happen?). She is also grateful to her sons, Stephen and Nick, for the wit, strength, and love they bring to her life. Special thanks to long-awaited "daughters" Orly and Megan, and to the new and lovely poetry in her life: Hawk and Skyler.

# About the Authors

Mary D. Esselman and Elizabeth Ash Vélez are friends, teachers, and poetry lovers whose books span the stages of women's lives.

Follow them on Facebook, Instagram, and Twitter @thenotsoyoung, and share your stories and poems about #agingwhilefemale and #howdidthishappen

For more info, visit www.agingwhilefemale.com